CORPORATE SHAIVISM

BALANCING POWER, PRECISION, AND PURPOSE

HARSHAL PATIL

Chennai • Bangalore

CLEVER FOX PUBLISHING
Chennai, India

Published by CLEVER FOX PUBLISHING 2024
Copyright © Harshal Patil 2024

All Rights Reserved.
ISBN: 978-93-56486-24-9

This book has been published with all reasonable efforts taken to make the material error-free after the consent of the author. No part of this book shall be used, reproduced in any manner whatsoever without written permission from the author, except in the case of brief quotations embodied in critical articles and reviews.

The Author of this book is solely responsible and liable for its content including but not limited to the views, representations, descriptions, statements, information, opinions and references ["Content"]. The Content of this book shall not constitute or be construed or deemed to reflect the opinion or expression of the Publisher or Editor. Neither the Publisher nor Editor endorse or approve the Content of this book or guarantee the reliability, accuracy or completeness of the Content published herein and do not make any representations or warranties of any kind, express or implied, including but not limited to the implied warranties of merchantability, fitness for a particular purpose. The Publisher and Editor shall not be liable whatsoever for any errors, omissions, whether such errors or omissions result from negligence, accident, or any other cause or claims for loss or damages of any kind, including without limitation, indirect or consequential loss or damage arising out of use, inability to use, or about the reliability, accuracy or sufficiency of the information contained in this book.

TABLE OF CONTENTS

Chapter 1. The Lingam Legacy: Foundational Principles for Organizational Stability 1

Chapter 2. Ardhanarishvara Approach: Embracing Diversity for Holistic Management 7

Chapter 3. The Nandi Narrative: Loyal Leadership and Team Building 14

Chapter 4. Rudraksha Relationships: Building Enduring Client Connections 22

Chapter 5. Trishul Tactics: Penetrating Market Defenses 28

Chapter 6. Panchakshara Principles: Mastering Marketing With Lord Shiva's Timeless Wisdom 34

Chapter 7. Shiva's Serenity: Mastering Emotional Intelligence in the Workplace 40

Chapter 8. Shiva's Silence: Mastering the Art of Listening in Communication 44

Chapter 9. The Mahadev Mindset: Embracing Invincibility and Resilience in Business 49

Table of Contents

Chapter 10. Third Eye Thinking: Harnessing Intuition for Strategic Decision-Making 54

Chapter 11. The Crescent Crown: Embracing Cycles of Business Growth and Innovation 60

Chapter 12. Mount Mandara Methodology: Stimulating Growth and Innovation in Business 68

Chapter 13. Ganga's Flow: Embracing Flexibility and Resilience in Business Strategy 75

Chapter 14. Ash's Assertion: Embracing Resilience and Transformation in Business 84

Chapter 15. The Tandava Turnaround: Orchestrating Transformative Business Moves 90

Chapter 16. The Blue-Throat Blueprint: Managing and Neutralizing Negative Influences in Business 100

Chapter 17. The Bhairava Balance: Mastering Risk Management and Bold Decision-Making 109

Chapter 18. The Vasuki Vantage: Mastering the Art of Negotiation in Business Deals 115

Chapter 19. Kailash Insights: Strategic Vision From the Summit 124

Chapter 20. The Himalayan Huddle: Elevating Team Dynamics to the Summit 131

Chapter 21. Focus on Inner Strength and Knowledge 150

🟤 Why I Am Writing This Book

In the bustling corridors of the corporate world, where every decision feels like a high-stakes game, I found myself searching for something more profound and enduring. My name is Harshal Patil, and I am the founder of BTB Venture, a company that has grown to remarkable heights.

Despite our achievements, I felt an inner void, a yearning for balance and deeper meaning in the relentless demands of corporate life and spiritual aspects. The world venerates business icons like Steve Jobs, and while their stories are inspiring, I realized I needed something different—something that resonated with my soul and provided a holistic approach to business and life.

During one particularly challenging period, I turned to spirituality, seeking wisdom that transcended conventional business strategies. This quest led me to the teachings of Lord Shiva. Intrigued by the profound depth of Shaivism, I began to delve into the ShriGuruGita, a sacred dialogue between Parvati and Shankar, and the core principles of Kashmir Shaivism. These ancient teachings opened my eyes to a new way of thinking and being.

💜 The Revelation

One fine day, while walking on the street early in the morning, I experienced a miraculous presence of Lord Shiva. This vision felt like a higher power guiding me toward a path that combined spirituality and business. It was a transformative moment that inspired me to integrate Shiva's teachings into my professional life.

I started to see the parallels between Shiva's spiritual principles and the values needed to thrive in the corporate world. The idea of blending these ancient pearls of wisdom with modern business practices was both exciting and daunting. I began taking baby steps to incorporate these principles into my daily routine. For instance, before starting my corporate day, I would invoke grace with a Shiva Stotram, setting a calm and focused tone for the hours ahead. I often played the serene sounds of Kailas' waters in the background, creating an environment of tranquility amidst the chaos.

🖤 The Embodiment of Business Principles

Through my journey, I realized that Kashmir Shaivism and the Shiva Sutras could serve as a great embodiment for businesses. These teachings offer timeless wisdom that, when incubated into business practices, not only brings joy but also elevates the entire organization. If Shiva is the center of the universe, then his principles can certainly be the center of a successful business and a fulfilled personality.

The Three Key Elements of My Journey:

1. State of Mind: Maintaining a balanced and centered mindset is crucial in the corporate world. Shiva's teachings emphasize inner peace and clarity, which are vital for making sound decisions and leading effectively. The Shiva Sutra "Caitanyamātmā" (Consciousness is the Self) taught me that by aligning my consciousness with my actions, I could achieve a harmonious and productive state of mind.

2. Intuitive Approach: Intuition plays a significant role in business. Shiva's principles teach us to trust our inner voice and harness the power of intuition to navigate complex situations. The Sutra "Cittaṃ mantraḥ" (The mind is the mantra) reinforced the idea that a focused and disciplined mind could serve as a powerful tool for business success.
3. Practical Approach: Beyond theory, this book provides practical steps to integrate these spiritual principles into everyday business practices, helping you build a resilient and thriving organization. The Sutra "Svadehe jagatsarvaṃ" (The entire universe exists within one's own body) inspired me to understand that true strategic insights come from within, enabling us to make decisions that align with our core values and goals.

The Power of Shiva's Teachings

As you read this book, you will discover how to merge the timeless wisdom of Lord Shiva with the dynamic demands of the corporate world. It is my hope that "Corporate Shaivism: Balancing Power, Precision, and Purpose" will not only inspire you but also equip you with the tools to create a business that is not only successful but also deeply meaningful.

Lord Shiva's stories can spark your instinct. For example, The story of Shiva's Silence highlights the profound impact of mastering the art of listening in fostering effective communication and creating a harmonious work environment. The principle "Jñānādhiṣṭhānaṃ mātṛkā," meaning "The foundation of knowledge is the source of all," emphasizes that true knowledge and understanding come from a solid foundation of attentive listening and comprehension.

In the ancient lore of Hindu mythology, Lord Shiva is often depicted as the ultimate yogi, deeply immersed in meditation. One such story highlights Shiva's ability to listen with profound depth and insight, which not only fosters wisdom but also creates a powerful impact on those around him.

Once, during a time of great turmoil, the Devas (gods) and Asuras (demons) were engaged in an endless conflict, causing immense suffering in the world. Seeking a resolution, they turned to Lord Shiva, known for his wisdom and impartial judgment. When they approached Shiva, they found him in deep meditation. His silence was profound, and his presence was commanding. The Devas and Asuras presented their grievances, expecting immediate action. However, Shiva remained silent, listening intently to every word.

His silence was not mere passivity; it was an active and powerful form of communication. By listening deeply, Shiva absorbed the essence of their words, understanding their fears, desires, and motivations. This deep listening allowed him to perceive the underlying issues causing the conflict.

After a long period of silence, Shiva opened his eyes and spoke with clarity and insight. His words were few but carried the weight of deep understanding and wisdom. He provided a solution that addressed the root causes of the conflict, leading to a lasting resolution. His ability to listen deeply and understand the core of the problem exemplified the true power of silent, attentive listening.

The principle "Jñānādhiṣṭhānaṃ mātṛkā" reminds us that the foundation of knowledge is essential for effective communication.

In a business context, this means that leaders and employees must cultivate the ability to listen deeply to understand and gain valuable insights.

By drawing on the profound teachings of Kashmir Shaivism and the Shiva Sutras, I have found a path that brings both joy and elevation. This journey has taught me that when these principles are at the heart of a business, the organization can achieve unparalleled success and fulfillment.

Conclusion

This book is the culmination of my journey—a journey that has transformed my approach to business and life. It is my way of sharing the lessons and insights that have guided me, blending spirituality with corporate life to find a harmonious balance. May it guide you, as it has guided me, to achieve greatness with grace and purpose.

In the end, the teachings of Lord Shiva offer a timeless legacy that transcends the boundaries of spirituality and business. By embracing these principles, we can build organizations that are not only resilient and successful but also deeply rooted in ethical values and spiritual wisdom. This holistic approach is the key to creating a legacy of balance, stability, and enduring success in the ever-changing landscape of the corporate world.

CHAPTER 1

THE LINGAM LEGACY: FOUNDATIONAL PRINCIPLES FOR ORGANIZATIONAL STABILITY

शिवसूत्र 1.1:

"चैतन्यमात्मा"

Caitanyamātmā (Consciousness is the Self)

The Lingam Legacy draws inspiration from the profound symbolism of the Shiva Lingam—a powerful representation of Lord Shiva. This legacy emphasizes the importance of establishing foundational principles that foster organizational stability and endurance. By focusing on core values, building strong foundations, and maintaining a long-term vision, businesses can achieve sustained success and resilience.

In the heart of an ancient city, there was a flourishing kingdom known for its wisdom and prosperity. The secret to its enduring stability lay in the teachings of an old sage who often spoke of the Shiva Sutras. Among the most profound was the sutra "Caitanyamātmā," meaning consciousness is the self. The king, wise beyond his years, interpreted this sutra as the foundation of his governance and organizational principles.

He believed that just as consciousness forms the core of human existence, a deep awareness and ethical integrity should form the foundation of his kingdom. He instilled this belief in his ministers and advisors, emphasizing that every decision should reflect the consciousness of the whole, not just individual desires. Under his rule, the kingdom thrived with peace and prosperity, embodying the principle that recognizing the divine in every action leads to stability and resilience. The citizens, aware of their interconnectedness, worked harmoniously, creating a society that stood strong through the tests of time.

In the ancient lore of Hindu mythology, Lord Shiva is often depicted as the ultimate source of balance and stability. One of the most profound symbols associated with him is the Shiva Lingam, which represents both creation and destruction, the endless cycle of life, and the stability that sustains it. It is said that the Lingam embodies the essence of Shiva's power, wisdom, and serenity, serving as a reminder that true strength comes from a solid foundation.

Once, when the world was in chaos, and the forces of darkness threatened to overwhelm, the gods sought Shiva's guidance. To restore balance, Shiva manifested the Lingam, demonstrating that stability and resilience are born from unwavering core values and principles. This act not only restored order but also established a lasting legacy of strength and endurance. Drawing inspiration from this timeless story, we can learn how to build and sustain a thriving organization in the ever-changing landscape of the corporate world.

🖤 Establishing Core Values

Framework:

1. Identify Core Values: Choose a set of timeless principles that reflect the essence of your organization.
2. Embed Values in Culture: Ensure these values are integral to daily operations and decision-making processes.
3. Communicate Values Consistently: Reinforce these values through internal and external communication.

Imagine a bustling technology firm at the dawn of the new millennium. The founders, driven by passion and ambition, recognized early on that to navigate the volatile tech landscape, they needed more than just cutting-edge innovation; they needed a set of core values that would anchor their organization through the storms of change. They chose three guiding principles: integrity, innovation, and customer focus.

Integrity was non-negotiable. Every product, every decision, every interaction had to reflect honesty and ethical standards. Innovation was the heartbeat of the company, driving them to constantly push boundaries and explore new frontiers. Customer focus ensured that their efforts were always aligned with the needs and desires of those they served. These values didn't just decorate the walls of their offices; they became the DNA of the organization, influencing every strategic move and operational choice. As a result, this tech firm not only survived the dot-com bust but emerged as a leader, renowned for its commitment to these enduring principles.

💚 Building a Strong Foundation

Framework:

1. Assess Risks: Conduct a thorough analysis of potential risks.
2. Allocate Resources Strategically: Ensure that all departments have the resources needed to operate effectively.
3. Develop Contingency Plans: Prepare for unexpected events with robust contingency strategies.

Consider a high-end restaurant chain known for its culinary excellence and impeccable service. The founders knew that maintaining their reputation required more than just great food; it needed a solid operational foundation. They invested heavily in training programs for their staff, ensuring every team member understood the importance of quality and consistency.

They also developed a comprehensive supply chain strategy, sourcing the finest ingredients from trusted suppliers and creating backup plans to handle disruptions. This approach wasn't just about operations; it was about delivering an exceptional dining experience that customers could rely on. The restaurant's meticulous attention to detail and proactive planning ensured they could maintain their high standards, even in times of crisis, building a loyal customer base and a strong market position.

💚 Long-term Vision

Framework:

1. Set Long-term Goals: Define clear, sustainable objectives for the future.
2. Adopt Sustainable Practices: Implement practices that promote environmental and social responsibility.
3. Monitor and Adapt: Continuously review and adjust strategies to align with long-term goals.

In the world of consumer goods, one company stands out for its unwavering commitment to sustainability. This company didn't just look at quarterly profits; it looked generations ahead. They adopted sustainable sourcing and production practices, ensuring that every step of their supply chain minimized environmental impact.

This wasn't just a business decision; it was a legacy. By focusing on long-term goals, they built a brand that consumers trusted and respected. Their products were not only high quality but also ethically produced, resonating with a growing market of environmentally conscious consumers. This long-term vision ensured that the company remained relevant and respected, regardless of market fluctuations.

💚 Conclusion

The Lingam Legacy in business management is about more than just survival; it's about thriving through stability and integrity. It involves embedding strong core values that define the organization's culture and character, building robust operational foundations that safeguard against unforeseen challenges, and maintaining a long-term vision that prioritizes sustainability and lasting success.

Through a structured framework and compelling stories, we see how businesses can not only endure but also flourish. By drawing from the ancient wisdom of the Shiva Lingam, modern organizations can create a legacy of resilience and excellence, navigating the complexities of the corporate world with a foundation as enduring and stable as the Lingam itself.

This approach to business management transforms abstract principles into tangible actions, creating a narrative that resonates with leaders and employees alike. It's about building an organization that not only stands the test of time but also inspires and uplifts everyone it touches.

CHAPTER 2

ARDHANARISHVARA APPROACH: EMBRACING DIVERSITY FOR HOLISTIC MANAGEMENT

"कृत्स्नं जगद् परमार्थतः"

Kṛtsnaṃ jagad paramārthataḥ (The entire universe is an expression of the Supreme Reality)

In the ancient lands of Bharat, nestled among the majestic Himalayas, there existed a kingdom that was renowned for its wisdom, prosperity, and harmonious way of life. The secret to this kingdom's enduring success lay in a profound and mystical teaching passed down through generations: the tale of Ardhanarishvara.

The Birth of Ardhanarishvara

Once, the great sage Bhringi, a staunch devotee of Lord Shiva, believed that only Shiva was worthy of worship and refused to acknowledge Parvati, Shiva's consort. This attitude deeply saddened Parvati, who represents Shakti (the divine feminine energy) and is an inseparable part of Shiva.

To enlighten Bhringi and the world about the fundamental unity and equality of masculine and feminine energies, Shiva and Parvati manifested as Ardhanarishvara—half male and half female. This divine form symbolized that both energies are essential and complementary, creating a perfect balance necessary for the universe's harmony.

The King's Vision

The story of Ardhanarishvara reached the ears of King Rajendra, a wise and just ruler of an ancient kingdom. Inspired by this profound symbolism, he began to see his kingdom's administration and management in a new light. He realized that just as the divine form of Ardhanarishvara embodies the balance of male and female principles, his kingdom too required a harmonious blend of diverse perspectives and strengths.

The Ardhanarishvara Approach is inspired by the composite form of Lord Shiva and Goddess Parvati, representing the synthesis of masculine and feminine energies. This holistic management concept emphasizes the importance of embracing diversity within the workplace to achieve balanced and effective decision-making.

In Hindu mythology, the Ardhanarishvara form of Lord Shiva, which is half male and half female, symbolizes the perfect union of masculine and feminine energies. This form represents the harmonious balance between strength and compassion, logic and intuition, power and nurturing. When the world was out of balance, and the gods needed guidance, Shiva and Parvati showed that true equilibrium is achieved through the integration of diverse qualities. By embodying both energies, they taught that embracing diversity leads to wholeness and harmony, a principle that can be profoundly applied in the modern corporate world.

♥ Integrating Diverse Perspectives: Framework for Personal and Corporate Application:

1. Encourage Diverse Leadership:
   - Personal: Seek mentorship and advice from a diverse group of individuals with varying backgrounds and experiences.
   - Corporate: Ensure leadership teams reflect a mix of genders, ethnicities, and backgrounds.
2. Create Inclusive Policies:
   - Personal: Adopt an inclusive mindset in personal relationships and networking, valuing different perspectives.
   - Corporate: Develop and implement policies that promote diversity and inclusion at all levels.
3. Foster Open Dialogue:
   - Personal: Engage in conversations with people from diverse backgrounds to broaden your understanding and perspectives.
   - Corporate: Encourage open and respectful communication among employees from diverse backgrounds.

Imagine a multinational corporation facing declining market share due to a lack of innovation. The leadership realized that their decision-making processes were dominated by a homogeneous group, leading to a narrow perspective on market needs and trends. In response, they formed a diversity council comprised of employees from various demographics, including different genders, ethnicities, and cultural backgrounds.

This council was empowered to influence major strategic decisions. The result was a more inclusive product development strategy that resonated with a broader customer base. By integrating diverse perspectives, the company not only revitalized its product offerings but also gained a competitive edge in the global market.

Use Case 1:

A large financial services firm recognized that its predominantly male leadership team was not fully addressing the needs of its diverse client base. They initiated a mentorship program aimed at developing female leaders within the company. Over time, the inclusion of more women in leadership roles led to more comprehensive financial solutions that catered to a wider range of clients. This shift not only improved client satisfaction but also increased market share and profitability.

Challenges Faced:

- Resistance to Change: Many established leaders were initially resistant to the idea of diversifying the leadership team, fearing it might disrupt the status quo.
- Cultural Barriers: Overcoming deep-seated cultural biases and stereotypes required persistent effort and sensitive handling.
- Maintaining Consistency: Ensuring that diversity policies were consistently applied across all departments and levels of the organization was a significant challenge.

♥ Enhancing Team Dynamics

Framework for Personal and Corporate Application:

1. Balance Skill Sets and Personalities:
   - Personal: Develop a balance of analytical and creative skills in your personal development and projects.
   - Corporate: Form teams with a mix of analytical and creative individuals.
2. Promote Collaborative Culture:
   - Personal: Foster a spirit of collaboration and mutual respect in personal and professional relationships.
   - Corporate: Encourage teamwork and mutual respect among team members.
3. Leverage Strengths:
   - Personal: Identify and utilize your unique strengths and those of others in collaborative efforts.
   - Corporate: Identify and utilize the unique strengths of each team member.

Consider a tech startup struggling to bring innovative products to market. The leadership noticed that their teams were either too focused on analytical detail or too inclined towards creative brainstorming, but lacked a balanced approach. They decided to restructure their teams to include both analytical thinkers and creative minds.

This new team composition led to a dynamic and synergistic work environment where detailed precision met creative innovation. Projects that once took months to complete were now delivered in weeks, with enhanced quality and market relevance. The balanced team dynamics not only improved project outcomes but also fostered a culture of collaboration and mutual respect.

Use Case 2:

A marketing firm sought to improve its campaign success rates. They restructured their teams to balance data analysts with creative designers and marketers. This diverse mix led to data-driven creative strategies that were both innovative and effective. As a result, the firm saw a significant increase in client satisfaction and campaign success rates, ultimately boosting its reputation and client base.

Challenges Faced:

- Integration Issues: Balancing diverse skill sets and personalities sometimes led to initial conflicts and misunderstandings within teams.
- Communication Barriers: Ensuring effective communication among team members with different working styles and backgrounds required continuous effort.
- Aligning Goals: Aligning individual team members' goals with the overall objectives of the team and organization was challenging but essential for cohesion.

♥ Conclusion

Embracing the Ardhanarishvara Approach in management involves recognizing the value of both masculine and feminine qualities, leading to a more balanced, inclusive, and effective organizational culture. This approach not only enhances internal cooperation but also boosts the company's adaptability and competitiveness in the global market.

By integrating diverse perspectives and balancing team dynamics, organizations can foster innovation, improve problem-solving, and create a harmonious work environment. The Ardhanarishvara Approach teaches us that true strength lies in unity and diversity, guiding businesses toward sustainable success and resilience in an ever-changing world. This approach also encourages individuals to embrace and integrate diverse qualities in their personal development and professional relationships, leading to a more holistic and enriched life.

Recognizing and addressing the challenges in executing this approach is crucial for its success. By remaining committed to the principles of diversity and inclusion, organizations and individuals can overcome these obstacles and achieve lasting, meaningful progress.

CHAPTER 3

THE NANDI NARRATIVE: LOYAL LEADERSHIP AND TEAM BUILDING

"चित्तं मंत्रः" Cittaṃ mantraḥ (The mind is the mantra)

In the tapestry of business leadership, the story of Nandi, the loyal bull and gatekeeper of Lord Shiva, offers profound insights into loyalty, steadfastness, and effective team building. Nandi's unwavering devotion and service to Shiva can be mirrored in the qualities of a good leader who fosters a cohesive and loyal team. Let's explore "The Nandi Narrative" and how it can be applied to leadership and team building in the business world.

In Hindu mythology, Nandi, the sacred bull, holds a special place as the devoted gatekeeper and companion of Lord Shiva. The bond between Shiva and Nandi is a testament to unwavering loyalty and dedication. One of the most famous stories illustrating Nandi's loyalty is when Shiva granted him the honor of always being by his side.

According to the legend, Nandi was born as the son of the sage Shilada. From a young age, Nandi was a devoted follower of Shiva. Pleased with Nandi's devotion, Shiva blessed him and made him the head of his ganas (attendants) and the gatekeeper of Kailash, his abode. Nandi's unwavering dedication and service to Shiva exemplify the qualities of a loyal and steadfast follower. This story teaches that true loyalty and service are rewarded with trust and responsibility, a principle that holds great value in the corporate world.

In the vast tapestry of Hindu mythology, the stories of Lord Shiva (Mahadev) and his faithful companion, Nandi, offer profound lessons that transcend time. These tales are not just mythological narratives; they are rich sources of wisdom that can be applied to our personal lives and business practices. By exploring the virtues embodied by Mahadev and Nandi, we can gain insights into values that foster loyalty, integrity, leadership, and resilience.

Nandi, the divine bull, is more than just the vahana (vehicle) of Lord Shiva; he is the epitome of devotion, loyalty, and service. According to legend, Nandi was born from the union of the sage Shilada's penance and Shiva's blessing. Shilada performed severe austerities to have a child who would be immortal and eternally devoted to Lord Shiva. Pleased with his devotion, Shiva granted him Nandi, who was born with divine qualities and a heart full of unwavering devotion to Mahadev.

Nandi's loyalty was tested many times, but his dedication never wavered. He stood guard at the gates of Kailash, Shiva's abode, and served as a mediator between Shiva and his devotees. Nandi's constant presence and unwavering faithfulness symbolize the ultimate servitude and loyalty to a higher purpose.

Mahadev, or Lord Shiva, is known as the destroyer in the Hindu trinity, yet he embodies creation, preservation, and destruction. He is the master of balance and the lord of the dance (Nataraja), symbolizing the rhythm of the universe. Shiva's meditative nature, his role as a family man, and his fierce aspects like Bhairava and Rudra demonstrate his multifaceted personality.

Values from Nandi and Mahadev

1. Loyalty and Devotion (Nandi):
   - Value: Unwavering loyalty and devotion are paramount.
   - Application: In business, this translates to employee loyalty and dedication to the company's mission. Employees who are devoted to their roles and the organization contribute significantly to its success. Cultivating a culture of mutual respect and loyalty ensures a stable and motivated workforce.
2. Integrity and Trustworthiness (Nandi):
   - Value: Being a trustworthy guardian and mediator.
   - Application: Integrity is the cornerstone of any successful business. Trustworthiness in leadership builds a reliable brand reputation and fosters long-term relationships with clients, partners, and employees.
3. Balance and Equanimity (Mahadev):
   - Value: Maintaining balance in creation, preservation, and destruction.
   - Application: Effective leaders balance various aspects of business management, from innovation and growth to

risk management and problem-solving. Equanimity in decision-making ensures sustainable growth and stability.
4. Resilience and Transformation (Mahadev):
   - Value: Embracing change and transformation.
   - Application: Businesses must adapt to changing market conditions and embrace innovation to thrive. Shiva's role as the destroyer teaches us the importance of letting go of outdated practices and transforming challenges into opportunities.
5. Meditative Focus and Clarity (Mahadev):
   - Value: Achieving clarity through meditation and introspection.
   - Application: Leaders who practice mindfulness and introspection can make clearer, more strategic decisions. A calm and focused mind is crucial for navigating the complexities of the corporate world.
6. Service and Protection (Nandi):
   - Value: Protecting and serving with dedication.
   - Application: A customer-centric approach, where the business is dedicated to serving and protecting its customers' interests, builds trust and loyalty. Providing excellent customer service and safeguarding clients' interests ensure long-term success.

Practical Lessons for Life and Business
Loyalty and Devotion:

- Story of Nandi: Nandi's unwavering loyalty to Shiva serves as a powerful example of the importance of dedication. In business, fostering a loyal workforce involves creating a

supportive environment, recognizing employee contributions, and aligning personal goals with organizational objectives.
- Practical Application: Implement employee recognition programs, provide opportunities for career growth, and ensure transparent communication to build a loyal and devoted team.

Integrity and Trustworthiness:

- Story of Nandi: As a mediator and guardian, Nandi exemplifies integrity and trust. Building a reputation of trustworthiness in business involves consistent ethical behavior and transparency.
- Practical Application: Establish a code of ethics, enforce accountability, and maintain transparency in all business dealings to build trust with stakeholders.

Balance and Equanimity:

- Story of Mahadev: Shiva's role in balancing creation, preservation, and destruction teaches us the importance of maintaining equilibrium. In business, this balance is reflected in managing growth while mitigating risks.
- Practical Application: Develop balanced business strategies that consider both short-term gains and long-term sustainability. Encourage a work-life balance for employees to maintain overall well-being.

Resilience and Transformation:

- Story of Mahadev: Shiva's ability to transform and adapt is crucial for overcoming obstacles. In business, resilience is essential for navigating market volatility and unforeseen challenges.

- Practical Application: Foster a culture of resilience by encouraging innovation, embracing change, and learning from failures. Develop contingency plans and invest in employee training to enhance adaptability.

Meditative Focus and Clarity:

- Story of Mahadev: Shiva's meditative nature provides insights into achieving clarity and focus. Leaders can benefit from mindfulness practices to enhance decision-making.
- Practical Application: Integrate mindfulness and meditation practices into the workplace. Encourage regular breaks and provide spaces for quiet reflection to improve focus and clarity.

Service and Protection:

- Story of Nandi: Nandi's dedication to serving and protecting reflects the importance of a customer-centric approach. Businesses that prioritize customer satisfaction build lasting relationships.
- Practical Application: Implement robust customer service programs, actively seek customer feedback, and ensure that products and services meet customer needs and expectations.

To integrate the values of loyalty, integrity, balance, resilience, focus, and service from the stories of Nandi and Mahadev into your business practices, follow this structured exercise:

Step 1: Identify Core Values

- **Exercise:** Gather your leadership team for a workshop.
  - **Activity:** Brainstorm and list the core values that define your organization. Use the values from Nandi and Mahadev

(loyalty, integrity, balance, resilience, focus, service) as a starting point.
- **Output:** A set of core values that reflect your organization's essence.

Step 2: Embed Values in Culture

- **Exercise:** Develop a plan to incorporate these values into daily operations.
  - **Activity:** Divide into groups and assign each group a value. Each group will create actionable steps to integrate their assigned value into the company's culture.
    - **Example:** For loyalty, develop employee recognition programs. For integrity, establish a code of ethics.
  - **Output:** A comprehensive plan with actionable steps for each value.

Step 3: Communicate Values Consistently

- **Exercise:** Create a communication strategy to reinforce these values.
  - **Activity:** Design internal and external communication materials that highlight your core values. This can include newsletters, posters, social media content, and training sessions.
  - **Output:** A communication plan that ensures all stakeholders are aware of and aligned with the company's core values.

Conclusion

The ancient stories of Nandi and Mahadev offer timeless wisdom that is highly relevant to modern business practices. By embodying the values of loyalty, integrity, balance, resilience, focus, and service, individuals and organizations can achieve greater success and fulfillment. These virtues not only enhance personal growth but also contribute to building a strong, ethical, and resilient business foundation.

Embracing the teachings of Nandi and Mahadev allows us to navigate the complexities of the corporate world with grace and purpose, fostering environments where both people and businesses can thrive.

CHAPTER 4

RUDRAKSHA RELATIONSHIPS: BUILDING ENDURING CLIENT CONNECTIONS

प्रत्यभिज्ञा हृदयम् 11:

"प्रकाशविमर्शमयोहि शिवः"

Prakāśavimarśamayo hi śivaḥ (Shiva is the union of consciousness and reflective awareness)

In a marketplace of an ancient city, a renowned merchant known for his wisdom and fairness had a secret to his enduring success. He often spoke of the verse from Pratyabhijna Hridayam, "Prakāśavimarśamayo hi śivaḥ," which meant that Shiva is the union of consciousness and reflective awareness.

He built his business relationships on this principle, believing that true connections are formed through deep understanding and reflective awareness. He took the time to understand his clients' needs and perspectives, fostering trust and loyalty.

His clients knew that they were more than just transactions to him; they were valued partners. This approach led to lasting relationships and a flourishing business, demonstrating that building enduring connections requires a foundation of mutual respect and reflective understanding.

In the unforgiving world of business, forging strong and lasting client relationships is not just important—it's essential. Drawing inspiration from the Rudraksha, a sacred bead revered in Hinduism and associated with Lord Shiva, businesses can cultivate "Rudraksha Relationships" characterized by durability, authenticity, and mutual respect. This article passionately explores how the profound qualities of the Rudraksha bead can be mirrored in exceptional client relationship management.

According to Hindu mythology, the Rudraksha beads originated from the tears of Lord Shiva. It is said that after a long period of intense meditation, Shiva opened his eyes and saw the suffering of humanity. Moved to tears by the pain and struggles of living beings, his tears fell to the earth and transformed into Rudraksha trees. The beads from these trees are considered sacred and are believed to possess the power to protect and bless those who wear them.

This story highlights Shiva's compassion and the protective power of the Rudraksha. Just as the Rudraksha beads are a manifestation of Shiva's empathy and strength, businesses can draw from these qualities to build client relationships that are resilient and nurturing.

The Seed of Authenticity: Genuine Connections

The Rudraksha is treasured for its authenticity and uniqueness, with each bead possessing a distinct configuration. In client relationships, authenticity is paramount. Businesses must strive for transparent and honest interactions, ensuring that communication transcends mere transactions and reflects a genuine commitment to understanding and meeting client needs.

Example: A marketing agency consistently provides clients with honest assessments of their campaigns, highlighting both strengths and areas for improvement, thereby fostering deep trust and respect.

KPIs to Track:

1. Client Satisfaction Scores: Regular surveys to gauge client happiness.
2. Client Retention Rate: Percentage of clients who continue services over time.
3. Net Promoter Score (NPS): Likelihood of clients recommending the business to others.

🖤 The Shield of Protection: Nurturing Trust

Just as the Rudraksha is believed to offer protection to its wearer, businesses should aim to safeguard their clients' interests. This involves proactively identifying potential issues, offering robust solutions, and ensuring that clients feel secure and supported throughout the partnership.

Example: A financial advisory firm diligently reviews clients' portfolios and provides timely advice to protect their investments, especially during volatile market conditions, thus reinforcing client trust.

KPIs to Track:

1. Incident Resolution Time: Time taken to address and resolve client issues.
2. Client Trust Index: Measured through feedback on perceived trustworthiness and reliability.
3. Number of Proactive Solutions Offered: Count of issues identified and resolved before client escalation.

♥ The Thread of Connection: Maintaining Communication

The Rudraksha bead is often strung on a thread, symbolizing connection. Maintaining open lines of communication is vital for building enduring client relationships. Regular check-ins, updates, and feedback sessions keep the relationship dynamic and responsive to clients' evolving needs.

Example: A software development company establishes bi-weekly calls with clients to discuss project progress, address concerns, and adapt to changing requirements, ensuring continuous alignment and satisfaction.

KPIs to Track:

1. Frequency of Communication: Number of touchpoints with clients per month.

2. Client Feedback Scores: Ratings from clients on communication effectiveness.
3. Response Time: Average time taken to respond to client inquiries.

🖤 The Facets of Versatility: Adapting to Client Needs

Each Rudraksha bead has a varying number of facets, representing its versatility. In business, being adaptable and flexible to meet diverse client needs is crucial. Recognizing that each client is unique and may require tailored solutions is key to building lasting relationships.

Example: A consulting firm offers customized service packages, understanding that each business has unique challenges and objectives, and thus needs a bespoke approach.

KPIs to Track:

1. Customization Rate: Percentage of services tailored to individual client needs.
2. Client Customization Satisfaction: Feedback on tailored solutions provided.
3. Number of Unique Solutions Developed: Count of bespoke solutions created for clients.

🖤 The Longevity of Commitment: Sustaining Relationships

Rudraksha beads are known for their durability, often lasting for years. In the context of client relationships, this translates to a long-term commitment to the client's success. Sustaining relationships beyond project completion or transactions demonstrates a dedication that clients deeply value.

Example: An event planning company maintains connections with clients even after the event, offering support for future events and demonstrating a commitment to long-term relationships.

KPIs to Track:

1. Long-term Client Retention: Duration of client relationships.
2. Repeat Business Rate: Percentage of clients who return for additional services.
3. Client Lifetime Value (CLV): Total revenue generated from a client over the duration of the relationship.

Conclusion

"Rudraksha Relationships" in business are about building connections that are authentic, protective, communicative, versatile, and enduring. By embodying the sacred qualities of the Rudraksha bead, companies can foster client relationships that stand the test of time, leading to mutual growth and success. Just as the Rudraksha holds a revered place in spirituality, these enduring relationships are the cornerstone of a thriving business.

By implementing these principles and tracking relevant KPIs, businesses can ensure they are continually improving their client relationship management strategies, leading to stronger, more resilient partnerships.

CHAPTER 5

TRISHUL TACTICS: PENETRATING MARKET DEFENSES

"स्वदेहे जगत्सर्वं"

Svadehe jagatsarvam (The entire universe exists within one's own body)

In the relentless battlefield of business, where competition is fierce and market defenses are formidable, leaders must arm themselves with strategies that not only penetrate barriers but also secure an unassailable stronghold. Drawing profound inspiration from Lord Shiva's Trishul—a symbol of destruction, protection, and unyielding willpower—businesses can adopt "Trishul Tactics" to dominate the market landscape. This article delves deeply into the synergy between the potent attributes of Shiva's Trishul and effective, aggressive business strategies.

The Trishul, or trident, is one of the most powerful symbols associated with Lord Shiva. It represents his ability to destroy evil and ignorance, protect his devotees, and maintain balance in the universe. The Trishul's three prongs symbolize the trinity of creation, preservation, and destruction—essential aspects of the cycle of life and the cosmos. In business, these principles can be mirrored in understanding the past, mastering the present, and anticipating the future.

One of the famous stories of Lord Shiva wielding his Trishul is during the battle against the demon king Tripurasura. The three cities of Tripura were floating fortresses of evil, causing havoc and suffering across the universe. Despite the formidable nature of these cities, Shiva remained calm and focused. With a single strike of his Trishul, he destroyed all three cities, restoring peace and balance.

This story illustrates the power of the Trishul to penetrate and eliminate seemingly insurmountable obstacles. It teaches us that with the right strategy and determination, any challenge can be overcome.

💚 The Three Prongs of Market Penetration

The Trishul, or trident, is a formidable weapon wielded by Lord Shiva, with each of its three prongs symbolizing the past, present, and future. In the context of business, this powerful trinity translates into a tripartite strategy for market penetration: understanding the past (market history), mastering the present (current market dynamics), and anticipating the future (emerging trends).

Understanding the Past: Market History

The first prong of the Trishul signifies the past. For businesses, this means conducting exhaustive market research to understand historical trends, past failures, and successes. This deep understanding helps in avoiding previous pitfalls and leveraging what has historically worked.

Example: A company aiming to enter the fiercely competitive smartphone market meticulously analyzes past trends to pinpoint successful features and designs, while also understanding the missteps that led to the downfall of previous players.

KPIs to Track:

1. Market Research Depth: Comprehensive analysis of past market data and trends.
2. Historical Success Replication: Frequency of incorporating past successful strategies.
3. Avoidance of Past Mistakes: Reduction in repeating past industry errors.

Mastering the Present: Current Market Dynamics

The second prong symbolizes the present. This involves a comprehensive understanding of the current market landscape, including competitor analysis, customer needs, and identifying market gaps. Mastering the present enables companies to position their products or services with precision.

Example: A retail brand conducts continuous surveys and utilizes social media analytics to accurately gauge current customer preferences, swiftly adapting its product line to meet the ever-evolving demands.

KPIs to Track:

1. Customer Feedback Scores: Regular feedback from current market consumers.
2. Competitor Analysis Reports: Frequency and depth of competitor analysis.
3. Market Gap Identification: Number of new market opportunities identified and exploited.

Anticipating the Future: Emerging Trends

The third prong represents the future. For businesses, this entails staying ahead by anticipating and adapting to emerging trends. Innovation and evolution are crucial for long-term dominance.

Example: An automotive company proactively invests in electric vehicle technology and autonomous driving features, positioning itself at the forefront of the inevitable shift towards sustainable and self-driving cars.

KPIs to Track:

1. Innovation Index: Number of innovative products or features developed.
2. Trend Adaptation Rate: Speed of integrating emerging trends into business strategy.
3. Future Market Readiness: Assessment of preparedness for future market changes.

♥ The Power of Will: Driving Forward

Beyond its three prongs, the Trishul embodies Shiva's indomitable will and determination. In business, this translates to relentless drive and resilience, crucial for penetrating market defenses and achieving lasting success. Companies must be unwavering in their efforts, constantly refining strategies and overcoming obstacles.

Example: A tech startup faces numerous challenges in a saturated market but remains resolute, continually iterating its product and business model until it secures its niche and gains significant market traction.

KPIs to Track:

1. Resilience Score: Measure of the company's ability to withstand market challenges.
2. Iteration Rate: Frequency of product and strategy iterations.
3. Market Penetration Success: Degree of market share gained over time.

In a time of great warriors and strategic minds, a young general sought to protect his kingdom from invading forces. He turned to the wisdom of the Shiva Sutras and found profound insight in the verse "Svadehe jagatsarvaṃ," understanding that the entire universe exists within one's own body.

He realized that to penetrate the defenses of his enemies, he first needed to understand his own strengths and weaknesses. By mastering self-awareness and harnessing his inner capabilities, he could develop strategies that were both innovative and effective.

With this deep insight, he devised tactics that anticipated his enemies' moves and exploited their vulnerabilities. His army, guided by his self-aware leadership, successfully defended the kingdom. This story became a legend, illustrating that true strategic prowess comes from understanding and mastering oneself.

Conclusion

The "Trishul Tactics" offer a robust approach to market penetration, inspired by the symbolic power of Lord Shiva's Trishul. By understanding the past, mastering the present, and anticipating the future—while harnessing an unyielding will—businesses can navigate market complexities and carve out a path to triumph. Just as the Trishul is a weapon of immense power and protection, these tactics equip companies with the necessary tools to break through barriers and safeguard their market position.

By embodying the resilience and strategic insight symbolized by Shiva's Trishul, businesses can achieve long-term success and dominance in their respective markets.

CHAPTER 6

PANCHAKSHARA PRINCIPLES: MASTERING MARKETING WITH LORD SHIVA'S TIMELESS WISDOM

"ज्ञानं बन्धः"

Jñānaṃ bandhaḥ (Knowledge is bondage)

Inspired by the sacred Panchakshara mantra, which embodies the essence of transformation and purity in spirituality, the "Panchakshara Principles" are designed to guide marketers toward creating more effective, resonant, and ethical campaigns. These principles focus on foundational aspects of marketing that resonate with core values: clarity, authenticity, adaptability, relevance, and sustainability.

Understanding the Panchakshara Principles:
📌 1. Clarity (Na)

Clarity in marketing means delivering messages in a straightforward, understandable manner that resonates clearly with the target audience. It involves simplifying complex information to ensure that communication is direct and easy to digest.

Corporate Example: A tech company simplifies its product descriptions on its website and marketing materials, using less technical jargon and more consumer-friendly language, leading to an increase in product uptake by non-technical users.

Relevance to Lord Shiva: In the myth of the churning of the ocean (Samudra Manthan), when the deadly poison Halahala emerged, it was Lord Shiva who stepped forward to consume it, thus saving the world. His clarity of purpose and action in this critical moment resonates with the need for clarity in marketing—where clear, decisive messaging can save a brand from drowning in complexity.

🔱 2. Authenticity (Ma)

Authenticity involves being true to the brand's values and promises, ensuring that all marketing messages align with the company's core beliefs and practices. This fosters trust and loyalty among customers.

Corporate Example: A clothing brand consistently promotes its commitment to sustainability by using ethically sourced materials and transparently sharing its supply chain processes.

Relevance to Lord Shiva: Shiva's authenticity is legendary. Whether he is the ascetic yogi or the family man, he stays true to his essence. Similarly, brands that remain authentic to their core values foster deep trust and loyalty, much like the unwavering devotion of Shiva's followers.

📌 3. Adaptability (Śi)

Adaptability in marketing refers to the ability to change and evolve strategies based on consumer feedback and market trends. This dynamic approach allows marketers to stay relevant and competitive.

Corporate Example: A food and beverage company regularly updates its product flavors and packaging in response to emerging consumer trends and seasonal preferences.

Relevance to Lord Shiva: Shiva's dance, the Tandava, symbolizes cosmic cycles of creation and destruction, highlighting the need for adaptability. In the ever-changing landscape of the market, adaptability ensures that a brand can dance through the cycles of change and emerge stronger.

📌 4. Relevance (Vā)

Ensuring relevance means crafting messages and campaigns that are pertinent to the audience's needs and interests at the right time. Relevance is key to capturing and maintaining consumer attention.

Corporate Example: An auto manufacturer launches an ad campaign focusing on vehicle safety features during a period of rising consumer concerns about automotive safety.

Relevance to Lord Shiva: Shiva's relevance across ages—from the time of the Vedas to modern spirituality—shows his enduring connection with the essence of life. Similarly, relevant marketing ensures that a brand remains connected and vital to its audience's current needs and desires.

📌 5. Sustainability (Ya)

Sustainability in marketing not only refers to environmental considerations but also to creating long-term relationships with customers through ongoing engagement and consistent value delivery.

Corporate Example: A software company implements a customer loyalty program that rewards ongoing subscriptions and enhancements, encouraging long-term customer retention.

Relevance to Lord Shiva: Lord Shiva's act of holding the Ganga in his hair to prevent it from flooding the earth demonstrates sustainability. This act of balancing immense power with gentle control mirrors how businesses should approach sustainability—maintaining balance for long-term success.

Applying the Panchakshara Principles in Marketing Strategies:

📌 Strategy 1: Integrated Marketing Campaigns

By applying the Panchakshara Principles, a company can ensure its integrated marketing campaigns are clear, authentic, adaptable, relevant, and sustainable. This approach ensures consistency across all channels, enhancing brand perception.

📌 Strategy 2: Digital Marketing Innovations

In digital marketing, utilizing these principles helps in tailoring content for different platforms, ensuring it matches the unique characteristics and user expectations of each channel while maintaining the brand's voice and ethical standards.

📌 Strategy 3: Customer Relationship Management

Effective CRM systems are designed with these core values in mind, ensuring communications are personalized and relevant, fostering stronger customer connections, and enhancing customer satisfaction and loyalty.

📌 Strategy 4: Product Development and Marketing

Incorporating the Panchakshara Principles from the product development phase ensures that products meet market needs authentically and sustainably, with marketing strategies aligned from the outset.

📌 Strategy 5: Crisis Management in Marketing

During a crisis, adhering to these principles helps maintain brand integrity, ensuring that communications are clear, authentic, and relevant to the situation, thereby protecting the brand's long-term reputation.

In an era of great scholars and merchants, a wise marketer understood that superficial knowledge could often be misleading. He shared the wisdom of the Shiva Sutra "Jñānaṃ bandhaḥ," explaining that true knowledge goes beyond the surface and binds the seeker to deeper truths.

He applied this principle to his marketing strategies, ensuring that every campaign was built on authentic and profound knowledge of the market and customers. This approach created deep, lasting connections with the audience, as his marketing resonated with their true needs and desires.

His campaigns were not just about selling products but about sharing valuable insights and building trust. This deep understanding and authentic approach became the cornerstone of effective marketing, proving that true knowledge is the foundation of lasting success.

Conclusion

The Panchakshara Principles provide a foundational framework for developing marketing strategies that are not only effective but also ethical and sustainable. By embedding these core values into their operations, marketers can build brands that achieve lasting success and resonance with their audiences.

Just as Lord Shiva embodies transformation and purity through the Panchakshara mantra, marketers can transform their strategies and maintain the purity of intent by adhering to these principles. This powerful alignment ensures that marketing efforts are not only impactful but also deeply meaningful, leading to enduring success and growth in the ever-evolving marketplace.

CHAPTER 7

SHIVA'S SERENITY: MASTERING EMOTIONAL INTELLIGENCE IN THE WORKPLACE

"उद्यमो भैरवः"

Udyamo bhairavaḥ (The rising will is Bhairava)

Embracing the tranquil yet powerful demeanor of Lord Shiva, known for his deep serenity and mastery over his emotions, offers profound lessons for emotional intelligence in the workplace. This concept, "Shiva's Serenity," guides professionals to cultivate a calm, composed workplace atmosphere, enhancing decision-making, empathy, and teamwork.

Emotional intelligence, though widely understood among professionals, holds deeper layers of significance when contextualized through the wisdom of Lord Shiva. Recognizing, understanding, and managing our emotions, as well as those of others, translates into superior leadership, reduced conflicts, and heightened productivity.

🪶 Self-Awareness and Self-Regulation

Inspired by Shiva's introspection and control, self-awareness involves understanding one's emotions and the impact they have on others. Self-regulation allows one to control or redirect disruptive emotions and impulses, much like Shiva's controlled meditation states.

Corporate Example: A corporate executive uses self-regulation to remain calm during heated board meetings, leading to more productive discussions and respected leadership.

Relevance to Lord Shiva: In the mythological tale of Shiva consuming the poison Halahala during the churning of the ocean, his ability to remain calm and controlled amidst chaos saved the universe from destruction. This level of self-regulation and composure is paramount for leaders navigating high-stress corporate environments.

🪶 Empathy and Social Skills

Shiva's empathy towards his followers mirrors his ability to understand the emotional makeup of other people. Social skills refer to managing relationships to move people in desired directions, whether in leading change, building teams, or resolving conflicts.

Corporate Example: A customer service manager trains in empathy to better understand customer complaints, leading to higher satisfaction ratings and customer loyalty.

Relevance to Lord Shiva: Lord Shiva's compassion is evident in his willingness to help devotees, regardless of their past. His ability to connect deeply with his followers and understand their needs is a powerful demonstration of empathy and social skills. Similarly, leaders who practice empathy can build stronger, more cohesive teams.

Cultivating a Serene Workplace:

Adopting Shiva's serenity involves creating a supportive environment where employees feel valued and understood. This includes mindfulness training, stress management workshops, and encouraging open communications.

Corporate Example: A multinational corporation introduces quiet zones, meditation sessions, and open forums for employee grievances, creating a more harmonious and productive work environment.

Relevance to Lord Shiva: Shiva's abode, Mount Kailash, is a symbol of tranquility and peace, a sanctuary where he meditates and recharges. Creating a serene workplace where employees can find peace and focus mirrors Shiva's practice of retreating to Mount Kailash for introspection and calm.

Incorporating Kailash Serenity: Just as Mount Kailash provides a serene environment for Lord Shiva to meditate and maintain his calm, workplaces can incorporate elements of serenity through dedicated quiet zones, spaces for reflection, and natural elements that promote calmness and focus.

Corporate Example: A financial services company redesigns its office space to include a rooftop garden, meditation rooms, and relaxation areas inspired by natural landscapes, fostering an atmosphere of peace and productivity.

Conclusion

"Shiva's Serenity" in the workplace emphasizes the importance of emotional intelligence as a cornerstone for a thriving corporate culture. By mastering these skills, leaders and employees alike can foster a more engaging, empathetic, and effective workplace.

Relevance to Lord Shiva: Lord Shiva balances his roles with calm and precision, exemplified in various stories where he manages cosmic duties while maintaining inner peace. By embodying Shiva's serenity and the tranquil essence of Mount Kailash, professionals can navigate the complexities of modern work environments with grace and effectiveness, creating a corporate culture where emotional intelligence drives success and harmony.

CHAPTER 8

SHIVA'S SILENCE: MASTERING THE ART OF LISTENING IN COMMUNICATION

"सप्तमं वादसंपत्तिः"

Saptamaṃ vāda-sampattiḥ (The seventh state is the perfection of discourse)

Inspired by the meditative stillness of Lord Shiva, "Shiva's Silence" delves into the profound impact of listening in effective communication. This guide explores the importance of listening—not merely hearing—to foster deeper interpersonal relationships, enhance understanding, and drive superior outcomes in both personal and professional settings.

Listening is an active, complex process that transcends mere auditory reception, involving understanding, interpreting, and responding. Effective listening is critical for building trust, resolving conflicts, and making informed decisions.

The Levels of Listening

1. Cosmetic Listening: The most superficial level where the listener hears the words but is disengaged. Research shows that 64% of employees feel leaders do not hear their concerns adequately, often leading to disengagement and turnover.
2. Conversational Listening: More engaged than cosmetic, this involves partial attention and occasional responses but lacks full engagement. Studies indicate that conversational listening can lead to misunderstandings, with 47% of communication breakdowns attributed to this level.
3. Active Listening: Full engagement, attention to words, tone, and body language. It involves reflecting, clarifying, and empathizing. Research by the International Journal of Listening shows that active listening improves workplace productivity by 32% and reduces errors by 23%.
4. Deep Listening: Also known as empathetic listening, it is the most intense level, where the listener engages emotionally with the speaker. Harvard Business Review states that deep listening can enhance emotional connections in teams, increasing collaboration by 40%.

Theories of Listening

- Transactional Model of Communication: Emphasizes the reciprocal nature of listening, where it is part of a continuous give-and-take in communication. This model underscores that 70% of effective communication is listening, yet only 2% of professionals receive formal listening training.
- HURIER Model: Stands for Hearing, Understanding, Remembering, Interpreting, Evaluating, and Responding,

highlighting the sequential steps involved in effective listening. Studies suggest that applying the HURIER model can improve comprehension and retention by up to 60%.
- Active-Empathetic Listening Theory: Focuses on the listener's role in empathizing with the speaker to truly understand and engage with the communication. Empathetic listening is linked to higher job satisfaction, with a Gallup survey noting a 27% increase in job fulfillment when employees feel heard.

Applying Effective Listening

Framework for Effective Listening

1. Mindfulness: Engage in mindfulness practices to enhance present-moment awareness, which is crucial for active listening. Mindfulness training can increase attention spans by 16%, improving listening capabilities.
2. Feedback: Offer constructive feedback to demonstrate understanding. Effective feedback loops can increase team performance by 24%, according to the Center for Creative Leadership.
3. Questioning: Employ open-ended questions to delve deeper into conversations. The Socratic method of questioning has been shown to enhance critical thinking and problem-solving skills by 20%.
4. Body Language: Utilize non-verbal cues to show attentiveness. Non-verbal communication constitutes 55% of the overall message in face-to-face interactions, as per research by Albert Mehrabian.
5. Avoiding Interruptions: Refrain from interrupting the speaker to ensure they feel heard. Interruptions can disrupt

thought flow and reduce message clarity by 37%, according to communication studies.

Daily Practices to Enhance Listening Skills

Morning Meditation: Start the day with 10–15 minutes of meditation to center your mind and prepare for active listening throughout the day. Regular meditation can increase grey matter in the brain, enhancing cognitive functions and listening skills.

Mindful Meetings: During meetings, practice active listening by focusing on the speaker, avoiding distractions, and providing thoughtful feedback. Companies with mindful meeting practices report a 30% increase in meeting productivity.

Reflective Journaling: End each day by reflecting on your listening experiences. Document instances of effective and ineffective listening, aiming to identify patterns and areas for improvement.

Empathy Exercises: Engage in role-playing scenarios or active listening exercises to build empathy. Empathy training can enhance emotional intelligence scores by 26%, fostering better interpersonal relationships.

Non-Verbal Communication Practice: Pay attention to your body language and facial expressions while listening. Practice maintaining eye contact, nodding, and other non-verbal cues to show engagement. Effective non-verbal communication can enhance listener credibility by 34%.

The Serenity of Mount Kailash

Incorporating elements of Kailash Serenity into your listening practice can transform your communication approach. Just as

Mount Kailash provides a serene environment for Lord Shiva to meditate and maintain his calm, creating a peaceful internal environment can enhance your ability to listen deeply.

Example: Create a quiet space in your home or office for reflection and mindful listening, inspired by the tranquility of Mount Kailash. Implementing such serene environments can improve cognitive function and reduce stress levels by 20%.

Conclusion

"Shiva's Silence" teaches us that listening, akin to meditation, requires discipline, patience, and practice. By mastering listening skills, we can enhance communication effectiveness, understand deeper issues, and build stronger relationships. This guide underscores the silent yet immensely powerful role of listening in successful communication across all areas of life.

By integrating these complex frameworks and daily practices, professionals can cultivate the art of listening, leading to more meaningful interactions and a more harmonious workplace and personal life. Just as Lord Shiva's serene presence commands respect and devotion, mastering the art of listening can create a powerful and positive impact on those around us.

CHAPTER 9

THE MAHADEV MINDSET: EMBRACING INVINCIBILITY AND RESILIENCE IN BUSINESS

"योनिवर्गः कल्पना संकल्पः"

Yonivargaḥ kalpanā saṃkalpaḥ (The womb of desires is imagination and intention).

In the arena of business, where challenges are as constant as the changing seasons, adopting the "Mahadev Mindset" offers a paradigm of invincibility and resilience inspired by Lord Shiva, the great transformer. This mindset encourages business leaders to embrace change, harness resilience, and master strategic foresight in ways that echo the divine attributes of Mahadev.

Lord Shiva is revered not just as a destroyer but as a rebuilder, embodying the cycle of change—destruction followed by rejuvenation. For businesses, this translates into the courage to dismantle outdated structures and innovate boldly. By adopting this aspect of the Mahadev Mindset, companies can lead their industries through transformative innovation that anticipates future needs and sets new benchmarks.

Corporate Example: A leading automotive manufacturer anticipates the shift towards electric vehicles (EVs) and reallocates significant R&D resources to develop cutting-edge EV technologies, eventually leading the market and setting new industry standards.

Relevance to Lord Shiva: The story of Shiva consuming the poison Halahala to save the world during the churning of the ocean (Samudra Manthan) exemplifies transformation. Shiva's act transformed a deadly crisis into a manageable challenge, showcasing the ability to convert adversity into innovation.

Resilience is at the core of the Mahadev Mindset. It is about maintaining a calm, unshakeable core amidst the chaos of market fluctuations and competitive pressures. This involves not only enduring but thriving through challenges by adapting strategies that ensure long-term sustainability and growth.

Corporate Example: During a global financial crisis, a major bank focuses on digital transformation, enhancing online banking services and customer support, which allows it to not only survive but gain a larger customer base as competitors struggle.

Relevance to Lord Shiva: Shiva's meditative calm amidst the chaos of the universe illustrates resilience. His ability to remain composed while balancing cosmic duties provides a model for maintaining stability and strategic focus during business crises.

Strategic withdrawal is another significant element of Mahadev's approach. This involves knowing when to pull back, conserve resources, and when to re-enter the market with a stronger, more focused strategy. This can be critical in avoiding significant losses and preparing for a more robust future.

Corporate Example: A multinational retail chain, facing declining sales in several international markets, decides to withdraw from these regions. After restructuring and strengthening its e-commerce platforms, it re-enters these markets with a more viable, digital-first approach, capturing a larger share of the market than before.

Relevance to Lord Shiva: Shiva's periodic retreats to Mount Kailash for meditation exemplify strategic withdrawal. These retreats allow him to recharge and gain new insights, which can be paralleled to a company pulling back to restructure and strategize before re-entering the market stronger.

The Dance of Creation and Destruction: Harnessing Creative Destruction

Just as Lord Shiva's cosmic dance (Tandava) governs the cycle of creation and destruction in the universe, businesses can adopt this rhythmic flux through continuous innovation. This means regularly assessing and revamping offerings, entering new markets, or completely overhauling outdated business models.

Corporate Example: A traditional publishing house facing declining sales digitizes its entire archive and transitions into a digital media company, significantly expanding its reach and revenue streams through online subscriptions and global access.

Relevance to Lord Shiva: Shiva's Tandava symbolizes the cyclical nature of the universe, reflecting the necessity of letting go of the old to make way for the new. This concept of creative destruction is essential for businesses to stay relevant and competitive.

Conclusion

The Mahadev Mindset in business is about seeing challenges as opportunities for transformation. It encourages adopting a holistic approach that encompasses embracing transformative change, building resilience, knowing when to retreat, and leveraging creative destruction for continual growth and revitalization. By embodying these principles, companies can navigate the complexities of modern markets with the wisdom and strength of Mahadev, turning potential setbacks into strategic victories.

Framework for Implementing the Mahadev Mindset

1. Embrace Transformation:
    - Action: Regularly review and dismantle outdated processes.
    - Practice: Allocate resources to R&D and innovation.
    - Metric: Measure the percentage of revenue from new products/services.
2. Build Resilience:
    - Action: Develop robust crisis management and contingency plans.
    - Practice: Invest in employee training and development.
    - Metric: Monitor employee engagement and customer satisfaction scores during crises.
3. Strategic Retreat and Reentry:

- Action: Identify underperforming markets or segments for temporary withdrawal.
- Practice: Focus on core strengths and prepare for reentry.
- Metric: Track market share growth post-reentry.
4. Harness Creative Destruction:
    - Action: Encourage a culture of continuous improvement and innovation.
    - Practice: Regularly assess and revamp product lines.
    - Metric: Measure the frequency and impact of new product launches.

Daily Practices to Foster the Mahadev Mindset

Morning Reflection: Start the day with a few minutes of meditation or reflection to clear the mind and prepare for strategic thinking.

Innovation Meetings: Hold regular meetings dedicated to brainstorming and discussing innovative ideas.

Scenario Planning: Conduct scenario planning exercises to prepare for various market conditions and challenges.

Resilience Training: Implement training programs focused on building personal and organizational resilience.

By integrating these frameworks and practices, business leaders can cultivate the Mahadev Mindset, enabling their organizations to thrive in the face of adversity and continuously transform in alignment with market dynamics.

CHAPTER 10

THIRD EYE THINKING: HARNESSING INTUITION FOR STRATEGIC DECISION-MAKING

"शक्ति चक्र संधाने विश्वसंहारः"

Shakti chakra sandhāne viśvasaṃhāraḥ (By fixing the mind on the wheel of energy, the universe is absorbed)

Drawing on the metaphor of Lord Shiva's third eye, which represents higher wisdom and intuition, "Third Eye Thinking" encourages business leaders to harness their intuitive insights for strategic decision-making. This approach combines data-driven analysis with intuitive judgment to navigate complex business environments and anticipate future trends.

Intuitive insights, when balanced with empirical data, can lead to powerful decision-making strategies. Leaders who cultivate their intuition can often quickly assess situations, read between the lines, and respond to new challenges with innovative solutions.

Corporate Example: The CEO of a tech startup uses her intuition to pivot her business strategy, shifting focus from hardware to software solutions based on emerging market needs and internal team strengths, significantly increasing the company's market share.

Relevance to Lord Shiva: The legend of Shiva opening his third eye to destroy Kama, the god of desire, symbolizes the power of higher wisdom and intuition to cut through illusion and reveal deeper truths. Similarly, leaders who harness their intuition can see beyond the immediate data to understand underlying trends and opportunities.

Statistics:

- According to a study by the Harvard Business Review, 62% of successful executives rely on intuition to make strategic decisions.
- Research by the University of Cambridge suggests that incorporating intuitive thinking into decision-making processes can improve innovation outcomes by up to 20%.

Intuition is deeply linked to creativity. Encouraging intuitive thinking in teams can lead to more innovative ideas and solutions that purely data-driven approaches might overlook.

Corporate Example: An advertising firm encourages team members to use "freethinking" sessions where intuition and spontaneous ideas are prioritized, leading to a groundbreaking campaign that captures widespread attention and acclaim.

Relevance to Lord Shiva: Shiva's dance, the Tandava, represents the rhythm of the universe and the creative energy that flows through it. Encouraging intuitive and spontaneous creativity in business mirrors this cosmic dance, fostering an environment where innovative ideas can flourish.

Statistics:

- A survey by PwC found that 80% of CEOs believe creativity and intuition are critical to their company's success.
- According to the World Economic Forum, companies that foster a culture of creativity and intuition see a 1.5 times higher employee engagement rate.

Third Eye Thinking enables leaders to make decisions that are not only reactive to current issues but are also proactive in anticipating future opportunities and threats. It involves looking beyond the obvious to understand deeper trends and patterns.

Corporate Example: A financial services firm integrates intuitive thinking into its risk assessment process, allowing it to avoid significant losses during an economic downturn by preemptively adjusting its investment strategies.

Relevance to Lord Shiva: Shiva's third eye symbolizes foresight and the ability to perceive hidden truths. In business, this translates to a leader's ability to foresee market changes and prepare strategically for future challenges and opportunities.

Statistics:

- Gartner reports that companies incorporating intuitive thinking in their strategy development processes achieve a 30% higher success rate in new market entries.

- A study by McKinsey & Company shows that strategic decision-making blending intuition and data can lead to a 25% improvement in long-term company performance.

To effectively integrate Third Eye Thinking, organizations must create an environment conducive to deep work—a state of focused, distraction-free productivity that enables deep thinking and creative problem-solving.

💜 Creating a Deep Work Culture:

1. Structured Schedules: Implement structured schedules that allocate specific times for deep work. Encourage employees to block out periods for uninterrupted focus.
2. Minimize Distractions: Design office spaces that minimize distractions, such as quiet zones or dedicated deep work areas. Use technology to reduce unnecessary interruptions.
3. Encourage Reflection: Promote regular reflection periods where employees can process their thoughts and ideas. This could include daily or weekly journaling and debriefing sessions.
4. Set Clear Goals: Ensure that deep work sessions are goal-oriented with clear, measurable outcomes. This helps maintain focus and track progress.

Corporate Example: A leading software development company designates "Focus Fridays," where no meetings are scheduled, allowing employees to concentrate on deep work. This initiative has resulted in a 30% increase in productivity and higher job satisfaction.

Statistics:

- Research by Cal Newport, author of "Deep Work," indicates that workers who regularly engage in deep work are 40% more productive than those who do not.
- A study by the University of California, Irvine, found that employees spend an average of 23 minutes recovering from interruptions, highlighting the importance of minimizing distractions.

💚 Practical Tips for Implementing Third-Eye Thinking

1. Develop a Quiet Mind: Regular meditation and mindfulness practices can help leaders clear their minds, making space for intuitive insights. Studies show that meditation can increase grey matter density, enhancing cognitive functions related to intuition.
2. Encourage Freethinking Sessions: Allocate time for teams to brainstorm without constraints, allowing intuitive ideas to surface. This can be structured as "blue sky thinking" sessions where no idea is too outlandish.
3. Balance Data with Gut Feelings: Use data as a foundation but allow room for intuitive insights. This means trusting your gut when it signals a strong feeling about a decision, even if the data isn't entirely clear.
4. Reflect and Learn: After making decisions, reflect on the outcomes to understand how intuition played a role. This reflection can help hone intuitive skills and integrate them more effectively with analytical thinking.

5. Build a Diverse Team: Diversity in backgrounds and thinking styles can enhance the intuitive capabilities of a team. Different perspectives can trigger unique insights and foster a more comprehensive understanding of complex issues.

Conclusion

"Third Eye Thinking" in business is about integrating the power of intuition with analytical rigor. By doing so, leaders can enhance their foresight, innovate beyond conventional limits, and make decisions that steer their companies toward long-term success. This method acknowledges that while data provides the map, intuition can illuminate the path through uncharted territories.

By adopting these practices and frameworks, business leaders can cultivate Third Eye Thinking, enabling their organizations to navigate complexities with the clarity and wisdom inspired by Lord Shiva's third eye. This approach not only enhances decision-making but also fosters a culture of innovation and strategic foresight, ensuring sustained success in an ever-evolving market landscape. Embracing deep work at the organizational level further empowers teams to harness their full cognitive potential, driving both individual and collective growth.

CHAPTER 11

THE CRESCENT CROWN: EMBRACING CYCLES OF BUSINESS GROWTH AND INNOVATION

"सतत्व पुष्टिः" *Sattva puṣṭiḥ* (Nourishment of the pure essence)

Drawing from the symbolism of the crescent moon adorned by Lord Shiva, the "Crescent Crown" represents the cyclical nature of business growth and innovation. This model underscores the importance of adapting through various phases of development, each offering unique challenges and opportunities.

Businesses, like the new moon, start with a seed of an idea—barely visible yet full of potential. This phase is critical for laying down the foundational strategy and vision.

Corporate Example: A fintech startup begins by identifying a gap in micro-financing, spending months in ideation sessions to refine their business model.

Relevance to Lord Shiva: The crescent moon on Shiva's head signifies the birth of new ideas and the cyclical nature of time. Just as the new moon symbolizes new beginnings, the ideation phase in business is about cultivating fresh ideas and laying a solid foundation for future growth.

Statistics:

- According to a study by CB Insights, 42% of startups fail because there's no market need, highlighting the importance of thorough ideation and conceptualization.
- Research from the Kauffman Foundation shows that startups spending more time in the ideation phase are 20% more likely to succeed in the long run.

Waxing Crescent: Market Entry and Traction

As the moon starts to reveal itself, so does the business begin to enter the market. This phase focuses on early growth, customer acquisition, and initial feedback loops.

Corporate Example: An e-commerce platform launches with a select range of products, slowly expanding as it starts to see which categories are most popular among consumers.

Relevance to Lord Shiva: The waxing crescent represents the gradual emergence of new ventures. For businesses, this phase is about gaining initial traction and starting to make an impact in the market.

Statistics:

- A report by Startup Genome indicates that startups in the scaling phase grow 20 times faster than those still finding product-market fit.
- Customer acquisition costs can decrease by up to 50% when businesses successfully navigate the market entry phase, as per research by Forrester.

♥ First Quarter: Establishing Presence

Here, the business begins to establish a solid market presence. Efforts are amplified to scale up operations and increase market share.

Corporate Example: A health tech company, after a successful pilot project, expands its services nationwide, establishing partnerships with major hospitals.

Relevance to Lord Shiva: Just as the first quarter moon signifies growth and establishment, this phase in business is about solidifying presence and scaling operations.

Statistics:

- Scaling companies have been found to grow revenues eight times faster than their non-scaling peers, according to a study by the ScaleUp Institute.
- A survey by Deloitte reveals that 80% of high-growth companies prioritize scaling operations during this phase to maximize market presence.

♥ Waxing Gibbous: Optimization and Expansion

During this phase, businesses focus on optimizing processes and expanding reach. The goal is to build on the existing customer base and improve operational efficiency.

Corporate Example: A software company begins to offer its services in new languages and regional markets, optimizing its interface based on user feedback from these regions.

Relevance to Lord Shiva: The waxing gibbous moon, nearly full, symbolizes nearing completion and refinement. Businesses in this phase enhance their offerings and streamline operations for broader market reach.

Statistics:

- McKinsey & Company reports that companies focusing on process optimization see a 15% increase in operational efficiency.
- Expanding into new markets can boost revenue by up to 40%, as indicated by a study from the Boston Consulting Group.

♥ Full Moon: Maturity and Dominance

At its fullest, the business is at its peak influence and stability. The focus shifts to maintaining dominance, exploring new innovations, and diversifying products or services.

Corporate Example: A leading smartphone manufacturer, at its market peak, begins to invest in developing smart home devices to expand its product ecosystem.

Relevance to Lord Shiva: The full moon represents completeness and peak potential. For businesses, this is the phase of dominance and exploration of new avenues to sustain growth.

Statistics :

- Companies at the maturity phase typically see a stabilization in growth, with steady revenue streams and market share, as per a report by Bain & Company.
- Innovation during the maturity phase can lead to new revenue streams, contributing up to 30% of total revenue, according to a study by PwC.

🖤 Waning Moon: Reflection and Innovation

As the moon wanes, so might business growth without reinvention. This phase is about reflecting on past strategies, acknowledging what is and isn't working, and innovating to spark new growth cyc13es.

Corporate Example: A multinational beverage company notices a shift towards healthier options and starts investing in low-sugar and organic variants to revitalize its product line.

Relevance to Lord Shiva: The waning moon signifies introspection and the need for renewal. Businesses must reflect on their journey, discard outdated practices, and innovate to initiate new growth phases.

Statistics:

- Reflective practices and strategic pivots can improve a company's agility by 25%, as suggested by a study from the MIT Sloan Management Review.
- Investing in new product development during the waning phase can lead to a 20% increase in market share recovery, according to research by Harvard Business School.

Conclusion

The Crescent Crown model teaches businesses to recognize and embrace the natural cycles of growth and innovation, much like the phases of the moon. By understanding these stages, companies can better prepare for the challenges and opportunities each phase brings, ensuring sustainable growth and continued relevance in the market.

Framework for Implementing the Crescent Crown Model

1. Ideation and Conceptualization (New Moon):
   - Action: Engage in deep market research and brainstorming sessions.
   - Practice: Encourage cross-functional teams to contribute ideas.
   - Metric: Measure the number of viable concepts generated.

2. Market Entry and Traction (Waxing Crescent):
   - Action: Launch pilot projects or MVPs.
   - Practice: Collect and analyze customer feedback.

- Metric: Track customer acquisition rates and initial sales.

3. Establishing Presence (First Quarter):
   - Action: Scale operations and enhance marketing efforts.
   - Practice: Form strategic partnerships and alliances.
   - Metric: Monitor market share growth and brand recognition.

4. Optimization and Expansion (Waxing Gibbous):
   - Action: Optimize processes and expand into new markets.
   - Practice: Implement customer feedback to refine offerings.
   - Metric: Evaluate operational efficiency and market penetration.

5. Maturity and Dominance (Full Moon):
   - Action: Diversify product lines and explore new innovations.
   - Practice: Maintain leadership through continuous improvement.
   - Metric: Assess revenue stability and innovation impact.

6. Reflection and Innovation (Waning Moon):
   - Action: Reflect on past performance and pivot as needed.
   - Practice: Invest in R&D for new product development.
   - Metric: Measure the success of new initiatives and market adaptation.

Practical Tips for Embracing the Crescent Crown

1. Regular Strategy Reviews: Schedule periodic strategy sessions to assess which phase your business is in and plan accordingly.
2. Adaptability Training: Offer training programs to help employees develop adaptability and innovative thinking.

3. Feedback Loops: Establish continuous feedback loops with customers and stakeholders to guide the transition between phases.
4. Innovation Labs: Create dedicated spaces or teams focused on innovation and experimenting with new ideas.

By adopting the Crescent Crown model, businesses can align their growth strategies with the natural cycles of development, ensuring sustained success and resilience in an ever-changing market landscape. This approach fosters a culture of continuous improvement, adaptability, and strategic foresight, enabling organizations to thrive across all phases of their lifecycle.

CHAPTER 12

MOUNT MANDARA METHODOLOGY: STIMULATING GROWTH AND INNOVATION IN BUSINESS

"प्रमात्र प्रमेय परिणाम"

Pramātra prameya pariṇāma (The knower and the known evolve together)

Inspired by the mythological churning of the ocean by the gods and demons using Mount Mandara to obtain the elixir of immortality, the "Mount Mandara Methodology" symbolizes a strategic process to stimulate significant growth and innovation in business environments. This approach advocates for leveraging core strengths and diverse resources to unearth valuable opportunities, akin to extracting the elixir from the ocean of possibilities.

Just as gods and demons cooperatively used Mount Mandara, businesses can bring together diverse teams to churn out innovative solutions. This involves integrating varied perspectives, skills, and experiences to tackle complex problems and discover breakthrough ideas.

Corporate Example: At a global tech firm, the CEO decided to form cross-functional teams to brainstorm and develop a revolutionary new product. This initiative brought together technology and design experts from different departments within the company. Through collaborative sessions, the team combined their diverse skills and perspectives, leading to the creation of a product that significantly outperformed market expectations.

Relevance to Mount Mandara: In the myth, the gods and demons set aside their differences to achieve a common goal. Similarly, businesses must leverage the diversity of their teams to drive innovation and uncover unique solutions.

Statistics:

- According to a study by Deloitte, inclusive teams are 80% more likely to outperform their peers in team-based assessments.
- McKinsey & Company reports that companies with diverse executive teams are 33% more likely to outperform their competitors on profitability.

The churning required sustained effort and commitment, emphasizing the need for perseverance in business strategies. Companies must commit to long-term goals and continuously push for progress, even when immediate results are not visible.

Corporate Example: A pharmaceutical company invested years in research and development, enduring numerous failures and setbacks. The persistent efforts of their R&D team finally led to the discovery of a groundbreaking new drug. This long-term commitment not only resulted in a significant market breakthrough but also established the company as a leader in innovative drug solutions.

Relevance to Mount Mandara: The gods and demons churned the ocean for an extended period before they could obtain the elixir. This underscores the importance of sustained effort and commitment in achieving significant business milestones.

Statistics:

- A study by the Boston Consulting Group indicates that companies investing in long-term innovation strategies see a 25% increase in their market value.
- The Harvard Business Review notes that 70% of successful projects result from sustained efforts over several years.

The churning of Mount Mandara was not without its challenges, yet it led to the creation of several divine treasures before the elixir emerged. Similarly, businesses can extract valuable insights and innovations from the challenges they face during their growth processes.

Corporate Example: An e-commerce company faced challenges in understanding customer preferences. By leveraging data analytics, the company analyzed customer purchase patterns and feedback, leading to significant improvements in user experience and increased sales. These insights allowed the company to better tailor its offerings to meet customer needs, driving sustained growth.

Relevance to Mount Mandara: The mythological process yielded various treasures before the elixir was obtained, symbolizing that challenges and obstacles can provide valuable outcomes. Businesses must navigate and learn from these challenges to discover new opportunities.

Statistics:

- According to a report by PwC, companies that utilize data analytics to overcome challenges are 5 times more likely to make better, faster decisions.
- Gartner research shows that organizations that embrace challenges and adapt their strategies accordingly achieve a 20% increase in performance metrics.

Framework for Implementing the Mount Mandara Methodology

1. Leverage Diversity for Innovation:
   - Action: Form cross-functional and diverse teams.
   - Practice: Conduct regular brainstorming and innovation sessions.
   - Metric: Measure the number of innovative ideas generated and implemented.
   - Story: A global tech firm, struggling with stagnant product lines, formed a diverse innovation team. By bringing together engineers, designers, and marketers, they were able to create a groundbreaking new product that revitalized their market presence.
2. Commit to Sustained Effort:
   - Action: Set long-term goals and milestones.
   - Practice: Invest in continuous training and development.

- Metric: Track progress towards long-term goals and employee development.
- Story: A pharmaceutical company, facing multiple setbacks in drug development, maintained a steadfast commitment to R&D. Years of persistence paid off when they finally developed a revolutionary drug, securing their market leadership.

3. Extract Value from Challenges:
   - Action: Analyze challenges and setbacks thoroughly.
   - Practice: Use data analytics to identify patterns and insights.
   - Metric: Evaluate improvements in processes and outcomes post-challenge.
   - Story: An e-commerce company, struggling with customer retention, used data analytics to understand buying behaviors. The insights gained helped them refine their user experience, leading to a significant increase in customer loyalty and sales.

♥ Practical Tips for Implementing the Mount Mandara Methodology

1. Regular Innovation Sprints: Implement short, focused periods dedicated to brainstorming and developing new ideas across diverse teams.
   - Example: An automotive company holds quarterly innovation sprints where engineers, designers, and sales teams come together to brainstorm new features for upcoming models.

2. Long-term Vision Workshops: Hold workshops to align the team with the company's long-term vision, emphasizing the importance of sustained effort.
   - Example: A financial services firm conducts annual vision workshops to ensure all employees understand and are committed to the company's 10-year growth plan.
3. Challenge Reflection Sessions: After major projects or challenges, conduct reflection sessions to discuss what was learned and how these insights can be applied moving forward.
   - Example: A software development company holds post-mortem meetings after each project to analyze what went well and what could be improved, fostering a culture of continuous learning.
4. Diverse Collaboration Platforms: Utilize collaboration tools and platforms that facilitate cross-functional teamwork and idea sharing.
   - Example: A multinational corporation uses an online collaboration platform to connect employees from different departments and regions, encouraging the exchange of innovative ideas.

Conclusion

The Mount Mandara Methodology in business is about more than just seeking growth; it's about stirring the depths of the company's potential to bring up the 'elixir' of sustainable success. By embracing diversity, committing to continuous effort, and learning from challenges, businesses can achieve transformative growth and innovation.

In a kingdom known for its dedication to excellence, the ruler introduced the Mount Mandara Methodology. Inspired by the Spanda Kārikās verse "Pramātra prameya pariṇāma," he emphasized that growth comes from the interaction between the knower and the known.

He encouraged continuous effort and churning of ideas to extract the elixir of growth. By fostering collaboration and shared learning, the kingdom's enterprises flourished, continually evolving and achieving greatness.

This methodology demonstrated that true growth requires persistent effort and the harmonious evolution of knowledge and practice.

By adopting the Mount Mandara Methodology, businesses can align their growth strategies with the natural cycles of innovation and resilience, ensuring sustained success and adaptability in an ever-changing market landscape. This approach fosters a culture of continuous improvement, strategic foresight, and collaborative innovation, enabling organizations to thrive amidst challenges and seize new opportunities.

CHAPTER 13

GANGA'S FLOW: EMBRACING FLEXIBILITY AND RESILIENCE IN BUSINESS STRATEGY

"जाग्रत्स्वप्नसुषुप्तभेदे तुर्याभोगाः स्वमहिमा"

(The experience of the fourth state, beyond waking, dreaming, and deep sleep, is the glory of the Self)

The Ganges, or Ganga, revered as a sacred river in India, is an enduring symbol of purity, renewal, and adaptability. Flowing from the icy heights of the Himalayas and traversing through diverse landscapes, the Ganga embodies the ability to adapt, transform, and rejuvenate. This chapter explores how the flowing qualities of the Ganga can provide insightful analogies for flexibility and resilience in business strategy, enabling organizations to thrive in rapidly changing markets.

The Ganga's journey from the glaciers to the plains is one of constant learning and adaptation. For businesses, this represents the necessity of lifelong learning and the continuous adaptation of strategies in response to external changes. Just like the river that carves new paths through obstacles, companies must remain agile, continuously learning from market feedback and evolving trends.

Corporate Example: Tesla exemplifies continuous learning by constantly adapting its business strategies in response to technological advancements and shifting consumer preferences in the automotive industry.

Relevance to Ganga: The continuous journey of the Ganga, adjusting its course through various terrains, symbolizes the need for businesses to remain flexible and responsive to change.

Statistics:

- According to the Association for Talent Development, companies that emphasize continuous learning see 37% higher productivity.
- Research by Deloitte indicates that organizations with strong learning cultures have 46% higher employee engagement and retention rates.

The Confluence of Diverse Streams:

At various points in its course, the Ganga meets and merges with other rivers, symbolizing the integration of diverse ideas and disciplines. In business, this confluence represents the strategic advantage of cross-functional collaboration and the integration of diverse ideas to foster innovation.

Corporate Example: Apple's success can be attributed to its ability to integrate technology with design, merging different fields to create aesthetically pleasing yet highly functional products.

Relevance to Ganga: The merging of the Ganga with other rivers illustrates the enrichment that comes from combining diverse perspectives and expertise.

Statistics:

- McKinsey & Company reports that diverse teams are 35% more likely to outperform their peers.
- A study by the Boston Consulting Group found that companies with more diverse management teams have 19% higher revenues due to innovation.

The Sediment Enrichment: Nurturing Innovation:

As the Ganga flows, it enriches the soil along its banks, much like businesses need to nurture innovation by creating environments that support creative thinking and idea generation.

Corporate Example: Google's 20% time policy encourages employees to spend 20% of their time on projects they are passionate about, fostering an environment where innovation can flourish naturally.

Relevance to Ganga: The sediment deposited by the Ganga enriches the land, akin to how nurturing innovation can enrich a company's culture and drive growth.

Statistics:

- Companies that foster innovation see a 30% higher performance than those that do not, according to a report by PwC.
- Research by the University of Pennsylvania shows that innovative companies are twice as likely to create job growth.

The relentless flow of the Ganga, despite obstacles, teaches resilience in the face of adversity. Businesses face numerous challenges, from economic downturns to competitive pressures, and like the Ganga, they must develop the resilience to continue moving forward.

Corporate Example: JPMorgan Chase demonstrated resilience by adapting quickly during the financial crisis of 2008, and adjusting its risk management strategies to navigate troubled waters successfully.

Relevance to Ganga: The Ganga's persistence in flowing through various terrains despite obstacles is a powerful metaphor for business resilience.

The Ganga is traditionally seen as a purifying force, removing impurities and renewing itself. Similarly, businesses today face the need for ethical cleansing and renewal, particularly in industries plagued by mistrust and scandal.

Corporate Example: Patagonia stands out for its commitment to environmental ethics and sustainability, continually pushing for industry standards that promote ethical practices and environmental stewardship.

Relevance to Ganga: Just as the Ganga purifies and renews, businesses must cleanse unethical practices to maintain trust and integrity.

Statistics:

- A study by Ethisphere shows that ethical companies outperform their peers by 14.4% in market value.

- According to the Reputation Institute, companies with high ethical standards have 2.3 times greater brand loyalty.

As the Ganga reaches its delta, it spreads out, covering a vast area and nourishing a wide ecosystem. This stage of its journey symbolizes the potential for businesses to expand their reach and embrace inclusivity in their market strategies.

Corporate Example: Netflix has successfully navigated global markets by offering diverse content that caters to a wide array of cultural tastes and preferences.

Relevance to Ganga: The expansive reach of the Ganga's delta represents the importance of inclusivity and broad market penetration for businesses.

Statistics:

- Companies that embrace diversity and inclusivity in their market strategies are 70% more likely to capture new markets, according to a report by the Harvard Business Review.
- A McKinsey report found that inclusive companies are 1.7 times more likely to be innovation leaders in their market.

Framework for Implementing Ganga's Flow in Business Strategy

1. Stream of Continuous Learning:
    - Action: Encourage a culture of continuous learning and adaptation.
    - Practice: Provide ongoing training and development opportunities.

- Metric: Measure employee participation in learning programs and resulting performance improvements.
- Story: Tesla's ability to stay ahead in the automotive industry through continuous learning and adaptation.

2. Confluence of Diverse Streams:
   - Action: Promote cross-functional collaboration and idea exchange.
   - Practice: Create interdisciplinary teams to work on projects.
   - Metric: Track the number and success rate of collaborative projects.
   - Story: Apple's success in integrating technology and design to create innovative products.

3. Sediment Enrichment:
   - Action: Foster an environment that supports innovation.
   - Practice: Implement policies that encourage creative thinking, such as Google's 20% time.
   - Metric: Monitor the number of new ideas generated and their impact on the business.
   - Story: Google's 20% time policy leading to significant innovations.

4. Resilient Currents:
   - Action: Develop strategies to build resilience against adversity.
   - Practice: Regularly review and update risk management and contingency plans.
   - Metric: Assess the company's ability to adapt and recover from challenges.

- Story: JPMorgan Chase's successful navigation of the 2008 financial crisis.

5. Purifying Waters:
   - Action: Commit to ethical practices and corporate responsibility.
   - Practice: Establish and enforce a strong code of ethics and sustainability initiatives.
   - Metric: Evaluate the company's ethical performance and reputation.
   - Story: Patagonia's commitment to environmental ethics and sustainability.

6. Wide Delta:
   - Action: Expand market reach and embrace inclusivity.
   - Practice: Develop strategies to enter new markets and cater to diverse customer bases.
   - Metric: Measure market penetration and customer diversity.
   - Story: Netflix's success in capturing global markets with diverse content.

🖤 Practical Tips for Embracing Ganga's Flow

1. Lifelong Learning Programs: Implement continuous learning initiatives to keep employees updated on industry trends and skills.
   - Example: A tech company offering regular workshops and courses on emerging technologies and methodologies.
2. Cross-Functional Teams: Establish teams composed of members from various departments to foster innovation.

- Example: A retail company forming a team with marketing, finance, and operations experts to develop a new customer loyalty program.
3. Innovation Incubators: Create incubator programs within the company to support new ideas and projects.
    - Example: A healthcare company setting up an internal incubator to develop and test new medical devices and solutions.
4. Resilience Training: Provide training on resilience and adaptability to prepare employees for unexpected challenges.
    - Example: A financial services firm offering resilience workshops to help employees manage stress and adapt to market changes.
5. Ethical Audits: Conduct regular ethical audits to ensure compliance with corporate responsibility standards.
    - Example: A consumer goods company conducting annual audits to assess and improve its sustainability practices.
6. Inclusive Marketing Strategies: Develop marketing campaigns that reflect and cater to a diverse audience.
    - Example: An entertainment company creating content that represents various cultures and demographics to expand its global reach.

Conclusion

Emulating the fluid adaptability of the Ganga, businesses can navigate the complex currents of today's economic environment. By embracing continuous learning, fostering cross-disciplinary collaboration, nurturing innovation, building resilience, maintaining ethical standards, and expanding reach, companies can stay relevant and successful in dynamically changing markets. The lessons from the Ganga's flow encourage businesses to remain adaptable and responsive, turning challenges into opportunities for growth and transformation.

By adopting the principles symbolized by the Ganga, businesses can align their strategies with natural cycles of learning, innovation, resilience, and inclusivity. This holistic approach fosters a culture of continuous improvement and strategic foresight, enabling organizations to thrive in an ever-evolving market landscape.

CHAPTER 14

ASH'S ASSERTION: EMBRACING RESILIENCE AND TRANSFORMATION IN BUSINESS

"ज्ञानाधिष्ठानं मातृका"

Jñānādhiṣṭhānaṃ mātṛkā (The foundation of knowledge is the source of all)

"Ash's Assertion" encapsulates a robust philosophy inspired by the symbolic ashes Lord Shiva adorns, which epitomize resilience and the transformative power of embracing setbacks. In business, this approach advocates for recognizing failures as essential learning moments that pave the way for future success and innovation.

Organizations that embody Ash's Assertion promote a culture where failures are seen as opportunities for growth. Encouraging employees to take calculated risks without fear of repercussions builds a resilient workforce ready to innovate and drive the company forward.

Corporate Example: A multinational corporation implements a 'fail forward' initiative, allowing employees to present failed projects to leadership teams. This not only promotes transparency but also drives collective learning from each setback, fostering an environment where every failure is a stepping stone to success.

Relevance to Lord Shiva: The ashes that Shiva adorns symbolize the end of one cycle and the beginning of another, illustrating the concept of renewal and transformation. In business, this translates to recognizing and embracing failures as necessary steps toward innovation and success.

Statistics:

- According to the Harvard Business Review, companies that promote a culture of learning from failure are 30% more innovative.
- A study by Deloitte found that 92% of companies believe that fostering a culture of continuous learning and resilience is critical to long-term success.

Systematic Learning from Setbacks

Resilience in business is not just about bouncing back but also about systematically learning and adapting from past mistakes. Organizations should establish processes to analyze setbacks thoroughly and integrate those learnings into their strategic planning.

Corporate Example: An e-commerce giant uses advanced data analytics to study customer behavior post-failed marketing campaigns, adapting their strategies in real-time to better meet consumer needs and avoid future missteps.

Relevance to Lord Shiva: Just as the ashes represent the remnants of the past, businesses can use the remnants of their setbacks to fuel future growth. Systematically analyzing and learning from failures ensures that past mistakes are transformed into valuable lessons.

Statistics:

- A report by McKinsey & Company highlights that companies leveraging data analytics to learn from failures see a 20% improvement in decision-making.
- Research by the University of California, Berkeley, shows that organizations with structured failure analysis processes are 25% more effective at implementing corrective actions.

Strategic Adaptation and Innovation

Ash's Assertion stresses the importance of strategic adaptation, where companies proactively evolve by integrating the insights gained from past setbacks. This ongoing adaptation is crucial for sustaining innovation and maintaining a competitive edge.

Corporate Example: A leading software development company routinely revises its product development lifecycle to incorporate feedback from failed product launches, significantly improving the relevance and user-friendliness of its software.

Relevance to Lord Shiva: The concept of ashes transforming into something new mirrors the need for businesses to continuously adapt and innovate. By integrating learnings from setbacks, companies can ensure their strategies remain relevant and forward-thinking.

Statistics:

- According to the Boston Consulting Group, companies that continuously adapt their strategies based on past learnings outperform their peers by 30% in market share growth.
- A study by Gartner indicates that organizations focusing on strategic adaptation see a 25% increase in innovation rates.

Framework for Implementing Ash's Assertion

1. Cultivating a Resilient Mindset:
   - Action: Promote a culture where failures are viewed as learning opportunities.
   - Practice: Implement initiatives like 'fail forward' sessions where employees can present and discuss failed projects.
   - Metric: Track the number of learning sessions and the subsequent improvements in project success rates.
   - Story: A multinational corporation's 'fail forward' initiative leads to increased transparency and collective learning, resulting in more innovative project outcomes.

2. Systematic Learning from Setbacks:
   - Action: Establish processes to thoroughly analyze setbacks.
   - Practice: Use data analytics and post-mortem reviews to identify key learnings from failures.
   - Metric: Measure the implementation of corrective actions and their impact on future projects.

- Story: An e-commerce giant uses data analytics to adapt strategies post-failed campaigns, improving customer engagement and sales.

3. Strategic Adaptation and Innovation:
   - Action: Regularly update business strategies to incorporate insights from past failures.
   - Practice: Revise product development cycles and strategic plans based on feedback and analysis.
   - Metric: Evaluate the success of new strategies and product improvements.
   - Story: A software development company's routine revisions based on feedback from failed launches lead to more user-friendly and successful products.

Practical Tips for Embracing Ash's Assertion

1. Failure Debrief Sessions: Conduct regular sessions to debrief on failed projects and extract valuable lessons.
   - Example: A tech startup holds monthly debrief sessions where teams analyze what went wrong and brainstorm how to avoid similar pitfalls in the future.
2. Risk-Tolerant Environment: Foster an environment where employees feel safe to take calculated risks.
   - Example: An innovation lab within a manufacturing company encourages engineers to experiment with new materials and processes without fear of failure.
3. Continuous Feedback Loops: Implement continuous feedback mechanisms to gather insights and make real-time adjustments.

- Example: A marketing agency uses customer feedback loops to refine its campaigns continuously, ensuring they stay relevant and effective.
4. Adaptive Strategy Workshops: Hold workshops focused on strategic adaptation and innovation based on past experiences.
   - Example: A financial firm conducts bi-annual workshops to update its risk management strategies based on recent market trends and past performance.

Conclusion

Ash's Assertion offers a blueprint for businesses to establish a resilient foundation, where setbacks are valued as critical components of the growth process. By fostering a culture that embraces failures, encourages continuous learning, and adapts strategically, organizations can rise from challenges renewed and stronger, much like the phoenix rising from ashes. This methodology not only ensures survival in turbulent times but also equips companies with the agility to thrive and innovate.

By integrating the principles of Ash's Assertion, businesses can create an environment that values resilience, continuous learning, and strategic adaptation. This holistic approach fosters a culture of innovation and agility, enabling organizations to navigate challenges and seize new opportunities with confidence. Embracing failures as learning opportunities ensures that every setback contributes to the company's growth and long-term success.

CHAPTER 15

THE TANDAVA TURNAROUND: ORCHESTRATING TRANSFORMATIVE BUSINESS MOVES

"स्वातन्त्र्यम् विश्वसिद्धिदम्"

Svātantryam viśva-siddhidam (Freedom brings about universal accomplishment)

The Tandava, a divine dance performed by Lord Shiva, is a mesmerizing depiction of cosmic cycles, creation, and destruction. In the realm of business, the Tandava represents bold and transformative moves that have the power to reshape industries and drive organizational evolution. This chapter explores how the principles embodied in the Tandava can inspire and guide businesses to orchestrate transformative maneuvers that lead to sustainable growth and competitive advantage.

The Strategic Choreography

The Tandava is not merely a random dance but a meticulously choreographed performance, symbolizing the importance of strategic planning and execution in business. Just as each movement in the Tandava serves a specific purpose, businesses must carefully plan and execute their strategic moves to achieve desired outcomes.

Corporate Example: Disney's strategic acquisitions of Marvel Entertainment and Lucasfilm allowed the company to leverage iconic characters and franchises, expanding its entertainment empire and driving significant growth.

Relevance to Tandava: Each move in the Tandava is deliberate and purposeful, mirroring the need for businesses to execute well-planned strategies to achieve their objectives.

Statistics

- According to Harvard Business Review, companies with well-defined strategic plans are 2.3 times more likely to achieve their business goals.
- McKinsey & Company reports that strategic acquisitions can increase shareholder value by 6% to 12%.

The Disruptive Rhythm

The Tandava's rhythmic beats disrupt the status quo, signaling the need for businesses to embrace disruption and innovation. Disruptive business moves, such as the introduction of groundbreaking technologies or business models, can create seismic shifts in industries, challenging incumbents and paving the way for new market leaders.

Corporate Example: Uber's disruptive entry into the transportation industry revolutionized ride-sharing, fundamentally changing how people commute and travel.

Relevance to Tandava: The disruptive rhythm of the Tandava symbolizes the power of innovation to challenge existing norms and drive industry-wide changes.

Statistics

- A study by Clayton Christensen found that disruptive innovations can create new markets and significantly impact existing ones, often leading to exponential growth.
- According to the World Economic Forum, 70% of the top 10 global companies by market capitalization in 2020 were disruptors in their industries.

The Harmonious Fusion

In the Tandava, disparate elements seamlessly come together in a harmonious fusion, illustrating the potential for synergistic partnerships and collaborations in business. Strategic alliances and partnerships allow businesses to leverage complementary strengths and resources, accelerating growth and innovation.

Corporate Example: The partnership between Starbucks and Spotify integrates music streaming into the coffee shop experience, enhancing customer engagement and loyalty.

Relevance to Tandava: The harmonious fusion in the Tandava mirrors the benefits of strategic partnerships, where combining strengths can create greater value.

Statistics

- Research by Deloitte shows that strategic alliances can lead to a 25% increase in innovation and 15% faster time to market.

- A report by PwC indicates that businesses with strong partnerships grow revenue 2.9 times faster than those without.

The Transformative Leap

The Tandava includes moments of dramatic leaps and bounds, symbolizing the transformative leaps businesses must take to stay ahead in competitive markets. Transformative leaps can involve diversification into new markets, adoption of disruptive technologies, or strategic pivots in business models.

Corporate Example: Tesla's bold leap into the electric vehicle market disrupted the automotive industry, challenging conventional wisdom and accelerating the transition to sustainable transportation.

Relevance to Tandava: The dramatic leaps in the Tandava represent the significant risks and bold moves businesses must undertake to achieve transformative change.

Statistics

- According to the Boston Consulting Group, companies that make transformative leaps in their business strategies outperform their peers by 35% in market share growth.
- Gartner reports that businesses that embrace disruptive technologies are 50% more likely to be market leaders.

The Regenerative Cycle

Just as the Tandava is a cyclical dance of creation and destruction, businesses must embrace the regenerative cycle of innovation and reinvention to stay relevant in evolving markets. Continuous innovation, coupled with a willingness to adapt and reinvent, allows businesses to thrive amidst changing dynamics.

Corporate Example: Apple's iterative approach to product development, marked by regular updates and innovations, ensures that its products remain at the forefront of technology and consumer preferences.

Relevance to Tandava: The cyclical nature of the Tandava signifies the need for businesses to continually innovate and adapt to sustain long-term success.

Statistics

- A report by the World Intellectual Property Organization highlights that companies investing in continuous innovation see a 15% higher market valuation.
- Research by Forrester indicates that businesses practicing continuous innovation are 2.5 times more likely to outperform their competitors.

The Empowering Momentum

The Tandava generates momentum and energy that propels the dance forward, underscoring the importance of momentum in driving business success. Businesses must build and sustain momentum through proactive decision-making, agile execution, and relentless focus on goals.

Corporate Example: Amazon's relentless focus on customer satisfaction and innovation has fueled its momentum, allowing it to expand into diverse industries and dominate the e-commerce landscape.

Relevance to Tandava: The momentum in the Tandava symbolizes the dynamic energy and sustained efforts required for businesses to achieve and maintain success.

Statistics

- According to a study by Bain & Company, companies that maintain strong momentum see a 1.4 times higher revenue growth rate.
- The McKinsey Global Institute reports that businesses with agile execution frameworks are 30% more efficient in achieving their goals.

Framework for Implementing the Tandava Turnaround

1. **Strategic Choreography:**

   - Action: Develop and execute well-defined strategic plans.
   - Practice: Regularly review and adjust strategies based on market feedback.
   - Metric: Track the achievement of strategic goals and milestones.
   - Story: Disney's strategic acquisitions of Marvel and Lucasfilm to expand its entertainment empire.

2. **Disruptive Rhythm:**

   - Action: Embrace and drive disruptive innovation.
   - Practice: Invest in R&D and foster a culture of experimentation.

- Metric: Measure the impact of disruptive initiatives on market share and growth.
- Story: Uber's revolutionary approach to ride-sharing disrupting the transportation industry.

3. Harmonious Fusion:

- Action: Form strategic partnerships and alliances.
- Practice: Identify and collaborate with complementary businesses.
- Metric: Evaluate the success of partnerships in achieving business goals.
- Story: The Starbucks and Spotify partnership enhancing customer experience.

4. Transformative Leap:

- Action: Take bold, transformative steps to innovate and grow.
- Practice: Diversify offerings and enter new markets.
- Metric: Assess the impact of transformative moves on business growth.
- Story: Tesla's entry into the electric vehicle market transforming the automotive industry.

5. Regenerative Cycle:

- Action: Embrace continuous innovation and reinvention.
- Practice: Implement iterative product development and regular updates.
- Metric: Monitor the success of new innovations and adaptations.

- Story: Apple's iterative approach to product development ensuring market leadership.

6. Empowering Momentum:

- Action: Build and sustain business momentum.
- Practice: Focus on proactive decision-making and agile execution.
- Metric: Track progress towards achieving business goals and maintaining momentum.
- Story: Amazon's relentless pursuit of customer satisfaction and innovation driving its dominance.

Practical Tips for Embracing the Tandava Turnaround

1. Strategic Planning Workshops: Conduct workshops to develop and refine strategic plans.
   - Example: A manufacturing company holding annual strategic planning workshops to align on long-term goals and market opportunities.
2. Innovation Labs: Establish innovation labs to drive disruptive ideas and experimentation.
   - Example: A healthcare company creating an innovation lab to develop cutting-edge medical technologies.
3. Partnership Programs: Implement programs to identify and foster strategic partnerships.
   - Example: A tech firm launching a partnership program to collaborate with startups and leverage emerging technologies.
4. Transformation Projects: Initiate bold projects aimed at transformative growth.

- Example: An energy company investing in renewable energy projects to lead the transition to sustainable energy solutions.
5. Continuous Improvement Initiatives: Launch initiatives focused on iterative improvements and innovation.
    - Example: A retail company introducing continuous improvement programs to enhance customer experience and operational efficiency.
6. Agile Execution Frameworks: Develop frameworks to ensure agile and proactive execution of business strategies.
    - Example: A financial services firm adopting agile methodologies to streamline processes and improve responsiveness to market changes.

Conclusion

The Tandava Turnaround inspires businesses to orchestrate transformative moves that reshape industries, drive innovation, and create sustainable competitive advantage. By embracing strategic choreography, disruptive rhythm, harmonious fusion, transformative leaps, regenerative cycles, and empowering momentum, businesses can navigate the complexities of today's business environment with agility and foresight. The principles embodied in the Tandava offer a compelling framework for businesses to orchestrate bold and transformative maneuvers that propel them toward success in the ever-evolving marketplace.

By integrating these principles, businesses can align their strategies with the dynamic and transformative nature of the

Tandava, ensuring sustained growth and competitive advantage. This holistic approach fosters a culture of innovation, agility, and strategic foresight, enabling organizations to thrive in an ever-changing market landscape.

CHAPTER 16

THE BLUE-THROAT BLUEPRINT: MANAGING AND NEUTRALIZING NEGATIVE INFLUENCES IN BUSINESS

"मूले सम्यक्त्वम्"

Mūle samyaktvam (Perfection lies in the root)

Inspired by the story of Lord Shiva consuming poison to protect the universe, the "Blue-Throat Blueprint" symbolizes the capacity to manage and neutralize negative influences within a corporate setting. This strategic approach focuses on identifying, containing, and mitigating the impacts of potential corporate toxins—be they cultural, operational, or reputational.

In a corporate empire facing internal challenges, we introduced the Blue-Throat Blueprint. Drawing from the Shiva Sutra "Mūle samyaktvam," I emphasized that true perfection lies in addressing root causes.

We implemented strategies to hold and neutralize corporate toxins by tackling issues at our source. This approach ensured that problems were resolved effectively, maintaining the organization's integrity and health.

The Blue-Throat Blueprint became a model for other companies, showing that addressing root causes and maintaining core integrity are essential for long-term success and stability.

💜 Identifying Potential Toxins

Organizations must vigilantly identify elements that could undermine their integrity or productivity. This involves regular audits, feedback mechanisms, and transparent communication channels to detect issues early.

Corporate Example: A financial institution implements a whistleblower policy that encourages employees to report unethical behavior, effectively identifying potential risks before they escalate.

Relevance to Lord Shiva: Just as Shiva identified the poison during the churning of the ocean, businesses must have robust mechanisms to identify potential threats and toxins within their operations.

Statistics

- According to the Ethics & Compliance Initiative, companies with strong whistleblower policies experience 46% fewer incidences of fraud.

- A study by PwC indicates that early detection of risks through audits can reduce the impact of corporate scandals by up to 60%.

Containing Negative Impacts

Once identified, the next step is to contain these toxic elements to prevent further damage. This might include isolating problematic departments, revising harmful policies, or managing disruptive personnel.

Corporate Example: A tech company faces a scandal involving data privacy violations; it responds by isolating the affected unit and overhauling its data handling procedures to prevent future breaches.

Relevance to Lord Shiva: Shiva contained the poison in his throat, preventing it from spreading and causing harm. Similarly, businesses must act swiftly to contain identified threats to protect their overall health.

Statistics

- Research by McKinsey & Company shows that effective containment strategies can reduce the fallout from corporate crises by 40%.
- A report by the Harvard Business Review found that companies that quickly isolate and address issues recover 30% faster than those that do not.

Strengthening Organizational Immunity

Building resilience against toxins involves strengthening the corporate culture and operational procedures. This includes training programs, reinforcing core values, and embedding ethical guidelines deeply within the corporate structure.

Corporate Example: A multinational corporation launches a global ethics training program for all employees, reinforcing the company's commitment to integrity and corporate responsibility.

Relevance to Lord Shiva: Just as Shiva's act of containing the poison fortified the universe against its destructive potential, strengthening an organization's core values and procedures builds resilience against internal and external threats.

Statistics

- According to Deloitte, companies with comprehensive ethics training programs see a 15% increase in employee compliance and a 22% decrease in unethical behavior.
- A study by the Ethics Resource Center found that companies with strong ethical cultures experience 75% fewer misconduct incidents.

Implementing Recovery Mechanisms

Effective recovery mechanisms are essential to bounce back from disruptions caused by corporate toxins. This includes strategic plans for reputation management, customer engagement, and employee support.

Corporate Example: After a significant operational failure, a retail chain launches a customer satisfaction survey, followed by targeted promotions to rebuild trust and customer loyalty.

Relevance to Lord Shiva: After containing the poison, Shiva continued his divine duties, signifying the importance of recovery and continuity. Businesses must also implement robust recovery plans to restore normalcy and regain trust.

Statistics

- According to the Journal of Business Ethics, effective recovery strategies can enhance customer trust by up to 20%.
- A study by Bain & Company shows that businesses with strong recovery mechanisms can retain up to 90% of their customer base post-crisis.

Monitoring and Learning

Continuous monitoring and learning from past incidents ensure that the organization remains vigilant and improves over time. This involves setting up advanced analytics to track performance and sentiment, both internally and externally.

Corporate Example: An automotive company uses machine learning tools to monitor online reviews and social media chatter after a product recall, allowing them to quickly address consumer concerns and improve future products.

Relevance to Lord Shiva: Shiva's awareness and vigilance in the cosmic balance can be likened to the continuous monitoring and learning businesses must engage in to prevent and manage future threats.

Statistics

- Gartner reports that businesses using advanced analytics for monitoring and learning see a 30% improvement in risk management.
- According to Forrester, continuous learning from past incidents can reduce the likelihood of future crises by 50%.

Framework for Implementing the Blue-Throat Blueprint

1. Identifying Potential Toxins:
   - Action: Conduct regular audits and establish feedback mechanisms.
   - Practice: Implement whistleblower policies and transparent communication channels.
   - Metric: Track the number of issues identified and resolved.
   - Story: A financial institution's whistleblower policy effectively identifies and addresses unethical behavior, preventing larger scandals.
2. Containing Negative Impacts:
   - Action: Isolate and address toxic elements promptly.
   - Practice: Overhaul problematic policies and manage disruptive personnel.
   - Metric: Measure the time taken to contain issues and the effectiveness of containment strategies.
   - Story: A tech company's swift response to a data privacy scandal prevents further breaches and restores customer trust.

3. Strengthening Organizational Immunity:
   - Action: Implement comprehensive ethics training and reinforce core values.
   - Practice: Regularly update training programs and embed ethical guidelines.
   - Metric: Assess improvements in compliance and reductions in unethical behavior.
   - Story: A multinational corporation's global ethics training program significantly reduces incidents of misconduct.
4. Implementing Recovery Mechanisms:
   - Action: Develop and execute strategic recovery plans.
   - Practice: Engage in reputation management and customer support initiatives.
   - Metric: Evaluate the effectiveness of recovery strategies in restoring trust and normalcy.
   - Story: A retail chain's customer satisfaction survey and targeted promotions rebuild loyalty after an operational failure.
5. Monitoring and Learning:
   - Action: Set up advanced analytics for continuous monitoring.
   - Practice: Use data to learn from past incidents and improve future strategies.
   - Metric: Track performance improvements and reductions in crisis occurrences.
   - Story: An automotive company's use of machine learning tools to monitor feedback after a recall enhances product quality and customer satisfaction.

Practical Tips for Embracing the Blue-Throat Blueprint

1. Regular Ethical Audits: Conduct regular audits to identify potential ethical issues.
   - Example: A manufacturing company implements quarterly ethical audits to ensure compliance with industry standards.
2. Robust Feedback Systems: Establish systems for employees and customers to provide feedback.
   - Example: A service company introduces an anonymous feedback platform for employees to report concerns without fear of retribution.
3. Comprehensive Training Programs: Develop training programs focused on ethics and corporate responsibility.
   - Example: A healthcare firm launches a mandatory ethics training program for all employees to reinforce its commitment to integrity.
4. Strategic Crisis Management Plans: Create and regularly update crisis management plans to handle potential issues.
   - Example: An airline company develops a comprehensive crisis management plan to address potential operational failures and customer service disruptions.
5. Advanced Monitoring Tools: Utilize advanced analytics and monitoring tools to track performance and sentiment.
   - Example: A retail brand uses social media monitoring tools to track customer sentiment and address issues in real time.

Conclusion

The Blue-Throat Blueprint advocates for a proactive and protective approach in corporate management, drawing from the mythological example of Lord Shiva's sacrifice. By identifying, containing, and neutralizing corporate toxins, and learning from each incident, organizations can ensure their long-term health and success in a competitive business environment.

By integrating the principles of the Blue-Throat Blueprint, businesses can create a resilient framework that protects against internal and external threats. This approach fosters a culture of vigilance, ethical integrity, and continuous improvement, enabling organizations to navigate challenges effectively and sustain long-term growth and success.

CHAPTER 17

THE BHAIRAVA BALANCE: MASTERING RISK MANAGEMENT AND BOLD DECISION-MAKING

"ज्ञानमात्मनि स्थितम्"

Jñānamātmani sthitam (Knowledge is rooted in the Self)

The concept of "The Bhairava Balance" draws inspiration from the fierce form of Lord Shiva known as Bhairava, embodying the dual principles of bold action and protective wisdom. This methodology in business focuses on mastering the art of risk management while embracing bold decision-making, crucial for navigating competitive markets and seizing growth opportunities.

Embracing Calculated Risks

Bold decision-making involves taking calculated risks, where the potential for significant rewards justifies the inherent risks. This approach requires a deep understanding of market dynamics and a clear risk mitigation strategy.

Corporate Example: A pharmaceutical company invests heavily in a risky but revolutionary drug development program, which ultimately leads to a breakthrough medication that dominates the market.

Relevance to Bhairava: Just as Bhairava embodies boldness, businesses must take decisive actions, assessing and embracing calculated risks to achieve significant rewards.

Statistics

- According to a study by the Boston Consulting Group, companies that strategically embrace risks outperform their peers by 45% in revenue growth.
- A report by PwC indicates that 73% of high-performing companies are willing to take risks to innovate and grow.

Strategic Risk Management

Bhairava, as a protector, symbolizes the need for strong risk management frameworks that prevent potential threats from derailing business objectives. Strategic risk management involves identifying, analyzing, and mitigating risks in a way that aligns with the company's overall strategic goals.

Corporate Example: An international investment bank implements advanced analytics and machine learning models to identify potential financial risks earlier, enabling proactive management that supports aggressive investment strategies.

Relevance to Bhairava: Bhairava's protective nature highlights the importance of safeguarding the organization against potential threats through effective risk management.

Statistics

- McKinsey & Company reports that organizations with robust risk management frameworks are 30% more likely to achieve long-term success.
- A study by Deloitte found that advanced risk management practices can reduce the impact of financial losses by up to 40%.

Balancing Risk and Innovation

The Bhairava Balance is about not only managing risks but also using them as a lever for innovation. By understanding the risks fully, companies can use them to drive creative solutions, exploring new markets, and technologies confidently.

Corporate Example: A tech company uses its insights into cybersecurity risks to develop a new suite of cutting-edge security products, turning potential threats into a business opportunity that sets them apart from competitors.

Relevance to Bhairava: The balance of Bhairava's fierce and protective aspects mirrors the need for businesses to innovate while maintaining a vigilant approach to risk management.

Statistics

- According to a report by Gartner, companies that integrate risk management with innovation strategies are 50% more likely to lead their market segments.
- Research by Forrester shows that businesses using risk insights to drive innovation see a 20% increase in new product success rates.

Framework for Implementing the Bhairava Balance

1. Embracing Calculated Risks:
   - Action: Identify high-reward opportunities that align with strategic goals.
   - Practice: Develop a clear risk mitigation plan for each opportunity.
   - Metric: Track the success rate of high-risk initiatives and their impact on growth.
   - Story: A pharmaceutical company's investment in a risky drug development program leads to a market-dominating breakthrough medication.
2. Strategic Risk Management:
   - Action: Implement advanced analytics to identify and manage risks.
   - Practice: Regularly update risk management frameworks to reflect changing market dynamics.
   - Metric: Measure the effectiveness of risk management practices in preventing losses.
   - Story: An international investment bank's use of machine learning models to proactively manage financial risks supports aggressive investment strategies.

3. Balancing Risk and Innovation:
   - Action: Use risk insights to drive innovation and explore new markets.
   - Practice: Develop products and services that address identified risks.
   - Metric: Assess the success of innovative initiatives driven by risk insights.
   - Story: A tech company's development of cybersecurity products based on risk insights differentiates it from competitors.

Practical Tips for Embracing the Bhairava Balance

1. Risk Assessment Workshops: Conduct regular workshops to assess potential risks and opportunities.
   - Example: A manufacturing company holds quarterly risk assessment workshops to identify high-reward opportunities and develop mitigation strategies.
2. Advanced Analytics Implementation: Invest in advanced analytics tools to monitor and manage risks.
   - Example: A financial services firm uses predictive analytics to identify potential market risks and adjust investment strategies accordingly.
3. Innovation-Driven by Risk Insights: Encourage innovation teams to use risk insights in product development.
   - Example: A healthcare company develops new medical devices that address specific risks identified through market analysis.
4. Regular Framework Reviews: Periodically review and update risk management frameworks.

- Example: An energy company conducts annual reviews of its risk management frameworks to ensure they remain effective in changing market conditions.
5. Cross-Functional Risk Committees: Establish committees with members from various departments to oversee risk management and innovation initiatives.
    - Example: A retail company forms a cross-functional committee to integrate risk management insights into its strategic planning and product development.

Conclusion

The Bhairava Balance advocates for a bold yet prudent approach to business strategy, where risk is not just a factor to be minimized but a catalyst for innovation and market leadership. This balance enables companies to make decisive moves that can lead to substantial growth while ensuring that safeguards are in place to protect the organization's assets and reputation.

By integrating the principles of the Bhairava Balance, businesses can navigate the complexities of competitive markets with a strategic blend of bold action and protective wisdom. This approach fosters a culture of innovation, resilience, and strategic foresight, empowering organizations to seize growth opportunities while effectively managing potential risks. Embracing the Bhairava Balance ensures that companies can thrive in dynamic environments, turning risks into catalysts for success and maintaining a competitive edge.

CHAPTER 18

THE VASUKI VANTAGE: MASTERING THE ART OF NEGOTIATION IN BUSINESS DEALS

"चित्तं चित्तवत्"

Cittaṃ cittavat (The mind is consciousness)

Drawing inspiration from the mythological serpent Vasuki, used as a rope in the churning of the ocean to extract the nectar of immortality, "The Vasuki Vantage" embodies strategies for mastering the art of negotiation in complex business deals. This approach highlights the importance of resilience, strategic positioning, and mutual benefits in negotiations.

Understanding the Vasuki Vantage

1. Preparation: Laying the Groundwork
   Before entering any negotiation, thorough preparation is vital. Understand not only your needs and goals but also those of the other party.
   Corporate Example: A tech company preparing for a strategic partnership conducts in-depth research on the potential partner's business model, market position, and strategic goals to align their proposal accordingly.
2. Patience: Learning from Vasuki's Endurance
   Vasuki was pivotal in the churning process, demonstrating immense patience. In negotiations, patience can often lead to more favorable outcomes as it allows for the collection of more information and leverage.
   Corporate Example: A multinational corporation negotiating a long-term supply contract waits patiently for the supplier's financial report before finalizing terms, ensuring a better understanding of the supplier's capabilities and constraints.
3. Leverage: Utilizing Your Strengths
   Just as Vasuki was central to both parties in the myth, identify and utilize your unique strengths in negotiations to serve both sides effectively.
   Corporate Example: A leading pharmaceutical company uses its strong market position and advanced research capabilities as leverage to negotiate better terms in a joint venture.
4. Flexibility: Adapting to Situations
   The ability to adapt your strategies based on evolving situations can lead to better negotiation outcomes.

Corporate Example: An e-commerce platform adjusts its commission structure in response to vendor feedback during negotiations, leading to a more balanced and mutually beneficial agreement.

5. Communication: Clear and Concise

   Effective communication is key. Clearly articulate your goals and listen actively to the other party's needs and concerns.

   Corporate Example: A financial services firm ensures that all stakeholders clearly understand the terms and benefits of a new investment product through comprehensive presentations and Q&A sessions.

6. Mutual Benefits: Aim for Win-Win

   Successful negotiations often result in a win-win situation where both parties feel they have gained something of value.

   Corporate Example: A software company and a hardware manufacturer collaborate to create a bundled product offering, resulting in increased sales and market share for both parties.

7. Strategic Concessions: Knowing What to Give Up

   Sometimes, strategic concessions can facilitate a deal. Understand what you can afford to lose in order to gain more important benefits.

   Corporate Example: A telecom company agrees to a lower initial fee in exchange for a higher percentage of future profits in a licensing agreement.

8. Building Relationships: Beyond the Deal

   Negotiations are not just about the immediate deal but also about building relationships that can yield future benefits.

   Corporate Example: A logistics company fosters long-term relationships with key suppliers through regular communication and collaboration on efficiency improvements.

9. Ethics and Honesty: Building Trust

   Maintaining ethical standards and honesty builds trust and can lead to more sustainable business relationships.

   Corporate Example: An energy company commits to transparent reporting and ethical practices in all negotiations, enhancing its reputation and stakeholder trust.

10. Persistence: Stay the Course

    Negotiations can be prolonged. Maintaining persistence throughout can lead to eventual success.

    Corporate Example: A construction firm remains persistent in negotiating better payment terms over several months, ultimately securing a contract that supports its financial stability.

Applying the Vasuki Vantage in Corporate Scenarios

📌 Scenario 1: Mergers and Acquisitions

In a high-stakes M&A deal, leveraging detailed due diligence and understanding the synergy benefits can align both companies towards a mutual goal.

Example: A manufacturing giant conducts thorough due diligence and identifies key synergies before acquiring a competitor, ensuring a smooth integration and realizing significant cost savings.

📌 Scenario 2: Contract Negotiations

During contract negotiations, outlining clear terms and conditions, while remaining open to adjustments based on the vendor's feedback, can smooth the process.

Example: A retail chain negotiates flexible delivery schedules with suppliers to accommodate seasonal demand fluctuations, benefiting both parties.

📌 Scenario 3: Crisis Management

In crisis situations, quick thinking and flexibility can help renegotiate terms that salvage a project or partnership.

Example: A construction firm facing delays due to unforeseen circumstances negotiates revised project timelines and penalties, maintaining client relationships and project viability.

📌 Scenario 4: International Trade Deals

International negotiations require an understanding of cultural nuances and local business practices, enhancing communication and effectiveness.

Example: An automotive company successfully enters a new market by adapting its negotiation strategy to align with local business customs and regulatory requirements.

📌 Scenario 5: Labor Disputes

Addressing labor disputes with empathy and a fair approach can resolve conflicts in a way that respects workers' rights while ensuring operational continuity.

Example: A manufacturing company negotiates improved working conditions and benefits with its labor union, leading to a resolution that prevents strikes and maintains productivity.

Framework for Implementing the Vasuki Vantage

1. Preparation: Laying the Groundwork:
   - Action: Conduct thorough research and understand both parties' needs.
   - Practice: Develop a detailed negotiation plan and set clear objectives.
   - Metric: Measure the alignment of negotiation outcomes with initial goals.
   - Story: A tech company's detailed preparation leads to a successful strategic partnership.
2. Patience: Learning from Vasuki's Endurance:
   - Action: Allow time for information gathering and leverage building.
   - Practice: Avoid rushing decisions and remain calm under pressure.
   - Metric: Track negotiation timelines and outcomes related to patience.
   - Story: A corporation's patience during supply contract negotiations results in more favorable terms.
3. Leverage: Utilizing Your Strengths:
   - Action: Identify and highlight unique strengths in negotiations.
   - Practice: Use leverage points to create mutually beneficial deals.

- Metric: Assess the impact of leverage on negotiation success.
- Story: A pharmaceutical company's strategic leverage leads to market dominance.

4. Flexibility: Adapting to Situations:
   - Action: Adjust strategies based on evolving negotiation dynamics.
   - Practice: Stay open to alternative solutions and compromises.
   - Metric: Evaluate the effectiveness of adaptive strategies.
   - Story: An e-commerce platform's flexibility results in a balanced agreement.

5. Communication: Clear and Concise:
   - Action: Ensure clear articulation of goals and active listening.
   - Practice: Use effective communication techniques to enhance understanding.
   - Metric: Measure communication clarity and its impact on outcomes.
   - Story: A financial firm's clear communication secures stakeholder agreement.

6. Mutual Benefits: Aim for Win-Win:
   - Action: Focus on creating mutually beneficial outcomes.
   - Practice: Identify and align common interests.
   - Metric: Track the realization of mutual benefits in agreements.
   - Story: A software company's collaborative approach leads to a successful joint venture.

7. Strategic Concessions: Knowing What to Give Up:
   - Action: Identify areas where concessions can be made strategically.
   - Practice: Balance concessions with gains to achieve overall benefits.
   - Metric: Evaluate the impact of concessions on final deals.
   - Story: A telecom company's strategic concession secures a lucrative licensing agreement.
8. Building Relationships: Beyond the Deal:
   - Action: Focus on long-term relationship building.
   - Practice: Foster trust and collaboration beyond immediate negotiations.
   - Metric: Measure the strength and longevity of business relationships.
   - Story: A logistics company's relationship-building efforts lead to sustained supplier partnerships.
9. Ethics and Honesty: Building Trust:
   - Action: Maintain high ethical standards and honesty.
   - Practice: Ensure transparency and integrity in negotiations.
   - Metric: Track trust levels and their impact on negotiations.
   - Story: An energy company's ethical conduct enhances stakeholder trust.
10. Persistence: Stay the Course:
    - Action: Maintain persistence and commitment throughout negotiations.
    - Practice: Stay focused on long-term goals despite challenges.
    - Metric: Assess the role of persistence in achieving successful outcomes.

- Story: A construction firm's persistence secures favorable payment terms.

Practical Tips for Embracing the Vasuki Vantage

1. Detailed Preparation: Invest time in comprehensive research and planning before negotiations.
   - Example: A tech company conducts extensive market research to strengthen its negotiation position.
2. Building Patience: Develop the ability to remain patient and composed during lengthy negotiations.
   - Example: A manufacturing firm trains its negotiation team in patience and stress management techniques.
3. Leveraging Strengths: Identify and highlight unique strengths and advantages in negotiations.
   - Example: A biotech company leverages its innovative research capabilities to secure strategic partnerships.
4. Flexibility in Approach: Be prepared to adapt strategies and explore alternative solutions.
   - Example: A financial services firm remains flexible in negotiations to accommodate changing client needs.
5. Effective Communication: Ensure clear, concise

CHAPTER 19

KAILASH INSIGHTS: STRATEGIC VISION FROM THE SUMMIT

"समाधिः साक्षात्कारः"

Samādhiḥ sākṣātkāraḥ (Meditative absorption is direct realization)

Drawing inspiration from Mount Kailash, revered as the abode of Lord Shiva and a symbol of spiritual enlightenment, "Kailash Insights" embodies the principles of strategic vision, clarity, and foresight. This chapter explores how businesses can develop and harness a strategic vision to navigate complex landscapes, drive growth, and achieve long-term success.

Understanding Kailash Insights

1. Elevated Perspective: Seeing the Bigger Picture
   Just as Mount Kailash stands tall, offering a panoramic view of its surroundings, businesses must cultivate an elevated perspective to see the bigger picture. This involves understanding market

dynamics, industry trends, and competitive landscapes to make informed strategic decisions.

Corporate Example: A global consumer goods company conducts regular market analysis and competitive benchmarking to identify growth opportunities and potential threats, enabling it to stay ahead of the competition.

2. Clarity of Vision: Defining Clear Objectives

   Clarity of vision is crucial for guiding organizational efforts towards a common goal. Clearly defined objectives provide direction and help align resources and actions.

   Corporate Example: A technology company sets a clear vision to become a leader in artificial intelligence by 2030, with specific milestones and KPIs to track progress.

3. Strategic Foresight: Anticipating Future Trends

   Strategic foresight involves anticipating future market trends and disruptions. By staying ahead of industry changes, businesses can adapt and innovate proactively.

   Corporate Example: An automotive manufacturer invests in research and development for electric vehicles and autonomous driving technologies, anticipating a shift towards sustainable and autonomous transportation.

4. Innovation and Adaptability: Embracing Change

   Embracing change and fostering innovation are key to maintaining a competitive edge. Businesses must create a culture that encourages creative thinking and agility.

   Corporate Example: A retail giant continuously innovates its e-commerce platform to enhance customer experience and integrates AI-driven personalization to stay relevant in the digital age.

5. Sustainable Growth: Balancing Short-term and Long-term Goals

   Sustainable growth requires balancing short-term achievements with long-term vision. This involves prudent resource allocation and strategic planning to ensure enduring success.

   Corporate Example: A pharmaceutical company balances immediate product launches with long-term research initiatives, ensuring a steady pipeline of innovative treatments.

Applying Kailash Insights in Corporate Scenarios

📌 Scenario 1: Strategic Planning and Market Expansion

Leveraging a clear strategic vision, businesses can identify new markets and growth opportunities. This involves comprehensive market research and strategic planning to enter new regions or sectors.

Example: A beverage company conducts extensive market research to expand into emerging markets, tailoring its products to local preferences and regulatory requirements.

📌 Scenario 2: Technological Innovation and Leadership

By anticipating technological trends, companies can invest in innovation and maintain leadership in their industries. This requires a forward-thinking approach and continuous R&D investment.

Example: A semiconductor manufacturer invests in cutting-edge technologies and collaborates with leading tech firms to stay at the forefront of semiconductor innovation.

📌 Scenario 3: Organizational Alignment and Execution

A clear strategic vision helps align organizational efforts, ensuring that all departments work towards common goals. This alignment enhances efficiency and effectiveness in execution.

Example: A multinational corporation implements a strategic framework that aligns its global operations, ensuring cohesive efforts toward achieving its vision of sustainability leadership.

📌 Scenario 4: Risk Management and Resilience

Developing strategic foresight allows businesses to anticipate risks and build resilience. This involves proactive risk management and contingency planning to navigate uncertainties.

Example: A financial services firm develops robust risk management frameworks to anticipate market fluctuations and regulatory changes, ensuring stability and resilience.

📌 Scenario 5: Sustainable Development and Corporate Responsibility

Strategic vision encompasses sustainable development and corporate responsibility. Businesses must integrate sustainability into their core strategies to achieve long-term success.

Example: A fashion retailer commits to sustainable sourcing and production practices, aligning its business strategy with environmental and social responsibility goals.

Framework for Implementing Kailash Insights

1. Elevated Perspective:
   - Action: Conduct comprehensive market and competitive analysis.
   - Practice: Regularly review industry reports and benchmark against competitors.
   - Metric: Measure market share growth and competitive positioning.
   - Story: A consumer goods company's market analysis identifies growth opportunities, keeping it ahead of the competition.
2. Clarity of Vision:
   - Action: Define clear, long-term objectives and strategic goals.
   - Practice: Set specific milestones and KPIs to track progress.
   - Metric: Evaluate progress towards strategic objectives.
   - Story: A technology company's clear vision to lead in AI by 2030 drives focused efforts and innovation.
3. Strategic Foresight:
   - Action: Invest in R&D to anticipate future trends and disruptions.
   - Practice: Monitor emerging technologies and market shifts.
   - Metric: Track innovation milestones and market adaptability.
   - Story: An automotive manufacturer's investment in EVs and autonomous driving anticipates industry shifts.
4. Innovation and Adaptability:
   - Action: Foster a culture of innovation and agility.
   - Practice: Encourage creative thinking and flexible strategies.

- Metric: Measure innovation outputs and adaptability rates.
- Story: A retail giant's continuous e-commerce innovation enhances customer experience and market relevance.

5. Sustainable Growth:
   - Action: Balance short-term wins with long-term strategic planning.
   - Practice: Allocate resources prudently and strategically.
   - Metric: Assess the sustainability of growth initiatives.
   - Story: A pharmaceutical company's balanced approach ensures a steady pipeline of innovative treatments.

Practical Tips for Embracing Kailash Insights

1. Regular Strategic Reviews: Conduct periodic reviews of strategic plans and market positions.
   - Example: A tech firm holds quarterly strategic review meetings to ensure alignment with long-term goals.
2. Vision Workshops: Organize workshops to refine and communicate the company's vision and strategic goals.
   - Example: A global corporation conducts annual vision workshops with senior leadership to align on strategic priorities.
3. Innovation Hubs: Establish innovation hubs to drive R&D and creative solutions.
   - Example: A manufacturing company creates an innovation hub to explore new materials and production methods.
4. Sustainability Integration: Embed sustainability into core business strategies.

- Example: A consumer electronics company integrates eco-friendly practices into its product development and manufacturing processes.
5. Risk Management Frameworks: Develop comprehensive risk management frameworks to anticipate and mitigate potential threats.
   - Example: A financial firm implements advanced risk management tools to monitor and mitigate financial and operational risks.

Conclusion

Kailash Insights: Strategic Vision from the Summit emphasizes the importance of strategic foresight, clarity, and innovation in navigating complex business landscapes. By cultivating an elevated perspective, defining clear objectives, anticipating future trends, fostering innovation, and balancing sustainable growth, businesses can achieve long-term success and maintain a competitive edge.

By integrating these principles, businesses can align their strategies with the strategic foresight and clarity symbolized by Mount Kailash, ensuring sustainable growth and resilience in an ever-evolving market landscape. This holistic approach fosters a culture of continuous improvement, strategic foresight, and adaptability, empowering organizations to thrive amidst challenges and seize new opportunities for growth and innovation.

CHAPTER 20

THE HIMALAYAN HUDDLE: ELEVATING TEAM DYNAMICS TO THE SUMMIT

"आत्मसंवेधनं"

Atma-samvedanam (Self-awareness)

Inspired by the formidable and collaborative nature of the Himalayas, the "Himalayan Huddle" symbolizes the pinnacle of team dynamics, emphasizing unity, strength, and resilience. This approach fosters an environment where teams are more than just groups of individuals; they are integrated units that thrive on mutual trust, diverse perspectives, and a shared mission.

Core Principles of the Himalayan Huddle

1. Shared Vision and Goals:
   Like climbers aiming for the summit, teams must align around common objectives. This alignment transforms individual efforts into a collective endeavor.

Corporate Example: A biotech firm unifies its R&D and commercial teams under a common goal to bring a new drug to market, enhancing cross-functional cooperation and speeding up the development process.

2. Interdependence and Role Clarity:

Recognizing each member's unique contributions ensures that the whole team functions more effectively, much like an ecosystem where each element plays a critical role.

Corporate Example: An aerospace company maps out clear roles within its engineering teams, facilitating seamless integrations of systems designed by different groups.

3. Mutual Trust:

Trust is the foundation of high-performing teams. It's built through transparency, reliability, and open communication.

Corporate Example: A finance corporation implements an open-door policy with regular check-ins, which fosters a culture of trust and prompt resolution of issues.

4. Diverse Perspectives:

Leveraging diversity within teams leads to innovative solutions and enhances problem-solving capabilities.

Corporate Example: A consumer electronics company forms global virtual teams that bring together diverse cultural insights, leading to products that cater to a broader market.

5. Continuous Learning and Adaptation:

Teams that embrace learning and adaptability can respond swiftly to challenges and opportunities.

Corporate Example: An IT service provider adopts agile methodologies, allowing teams to learn from ongoing projects and adapt processes in real time for better outcomes.

6. Effective Conflict Management:
   Addressing and resolving conflicts constructively prevents them from undermining team cohesion.
   Corporate Example: A real estate agency trains its sales teams in negotiation and conflict resolution, improving collaboration and client interactions.
7. Distributed Leadership:
   When leadership is encouraged at every level, teams become more agile and responsive to changes.
   Corporate Example: A digital marketing agency implements a rotational leadership strategy where different team members lead weekly planning sessions.
8. Recognition and Reward:
   Acknowledging both individual achievements and team successes boosts morale and motivates continued excellence.
   Corporate Example: A retail chain introduces a peer-recognition program that celebrates employees who go above and beyond in teamwork and customer service.
9. Respect and Inclusivity:
   Cultivating an environment where every voice is heard and valued is crucial for sustaining engagement and enthusiasm.
   Corporate Example: A publishing house establishes a monthly forum where employees from all levels share ideas and feedback with top management.
10. Robust Communication Channels:
    Maintaining open lines of communication ensures that information flows freely, supporting better decision-making and coordination.

Corporate Example: A logistics company overhauls its internal communication tools to include instant messaging and project management software, enhancing real-time updates and collaboration.

Applying the Himalayan Huddle in Corporate Scenarios

📌 Scenario 1: Cross-Functional Project Teams

Leveraging shared vision and role clarity, cross-functional teams can drive complex projects to success by aligning efforts and integrating diverse skills.

Example: A tech startup forms a cross-functional team to develop a new app, ensuring that design, development, and marketing are seamlessly integrated.

📌 Scenario 2: Global Team Collaboration

By embracing diverse perspectives and robust communication channels, global teams can overcome cultural and geographical barriers to innovate and solve problems effectively.

Example: A multinational corporation uses virtual collaboration tools to bring together global teams, facilitating continuous innovation and problem-solving.

📌 Scenario 3: Organizational Change Management

During times of change, mutual trust, effective conflict management, and continuous learning can help teams navigate transitions smoothly.

Example: A healthcare provider undergoing digital transformation trains its staff in change management and conflict resolution to ensure a smooth transition.

📌 Scenario 4: Customer-Centric Teams

Teams focused on customer satisfaction can benefit from respect, inclusivity, and recognition, leading to higher engagement and better service.

Example: A hospitality company creates customer-centric teams that receive regular training and recognition, resulting in improved guest satisfaction.

📌 Scenario 5: Innovation Hubs

Establishing innovation hubs that emphasize interdependence, flexibility, and distributed leadership can drive breakthrough ideas and products.

Example: An automotive company sets up an innovation hub where engineers and designers collaborate on next-generation vehicle technologies.

Framework for Implementing the Himalayan Huddle

1. Shared Vision and Goals:
   - Action: Develop and communicate a clear vision and set of objectives.
   - Practice: Align team efforts towards common goals through regular updates and feedback.
   - Metric: Measure the alignment and progress towards shared objectives.

- Story: A biotech firm's unified goal accelerates drug development and market entry.
2. Interdependence and Role Clarity:
    - Action: Clearly define roles and responsibilities within the team.
    - Practice: Ensure each member understands their role and how it contributes to the team's success.
    - Metric: Track team efficiency and integration success rates.
    - Story: An aerospace company's clear role definitions lead to seamless system integrations.
3. Mutual Trust:
    - Action: Foster a culture of transparency and open communication.
    - Practice: Implement regular check-ins and an open-door policy.
    - Metric: Evaluate trust levels through employee surveys and retention rates.
    - Story: A finance corporation's open-door policy builds a culture of trust and prompt issue resolution.
4. Diverse Perspectives:
    - Action: Promote diversity within teams.
    - Practice: Create global virtual teams to leverage diverse insights.
    - Metric: Assess the impact of diversity on innovation and problem-solving.
    - Story: A consumer electronics company's diverse teams create products for a global market.

5. Continuous Learning and Adaptation:
   - Action: Encourage ongoing learning and adaptability.
   - Practice: Implement agile methodologies and continuous feedback loops.
   - Metric: Measure adaptability and learning outcomes.
   - Story: An IT service provider's agile practices lead to real-time process improvements.
6. Effective Conflict Management:
   - Action: Train teams in conflict resolution and negotiation.
   - Practice: Address conflicts constructively to maintain cohesion.
   - Metric: Track conflict resolution success rates and team satisfaction.
   - Story: A real estate agency's conflict resolution training improves team collaboration.
7. Distributed Leadership:
   - Action: Encourage leadership at all levels.
   - Practice: Implement rotational leadership roles within teams.
   - Metric: Evaluate leadership development and team responsiveness.
   - Story: A digital marketing agency's rotational leadership enhances team agility.
8. Recognition and Reward:
   - Action: Recognize and reward individual and team achievements.
   - Practice: Introduce peer-recognition programs and celebrate successes.
   - Metric: Measure morale and motivation levels.

- Story: A retail chain's peer-recognition program boosts teamwork and customer service.
9. Respect and Inclusivity:
    - Action: Cultivate an inclusive and respectful team environment.
    - Practice: Hold regular forums for idea-sharing and feedback.
    - Metric: Assess engagement and inclusivity through surveys and participation rates.
    - Story: A publishing house's monthly forum ensures all voices are heard and valued.
10. Robust Communication Channels:
    - Action: Implement effective communication tools and practices.
    - Practice: Use instant messaging and project management software for real-time updates.
    - Metric: Measure communication efficiency and coordination success.
    - Story: A logistics company's upgraded communication tools enhance real-time collaboration.

Practical Tips for Embracing the Himalayan Huddle

1. Team Vision Workshops: Conduct workshops to align team vision and goals.
    - Example: A biotech firm holds vision workshops to unify R&D and commercial teams.
2. Role Clarity Sessions: Organize sessions to clarify roles and responsibilities.

- Example: An aerospace company hosts role clarity sessions to ensure seamless team integration.
3. Trust-Building Activities: Implement activities to build mutual trust within teams.
    - Example: A finance corporation arranges trust-building exercises and regular check-ins.
4. Diversity and Inclusion Programs: Develop programs to promote diversity and inclusion.
    - Example: A consumer electronics company creates global virtual teams to enhance cultural insights.
5. Agile Methodologies: Adopt agile practices to enhance learning and adaptability.
    - Example: An IT service provider implements agile methodologies for real-time process improvements.
6. Conflict Resolution Training: Provide training in conflict management and negotiation.
    - Example: A real estate agency offers conflict resolution training to improve team collaboration.
7. Leadership Development Programs: Encourage leadership at all levels through development programs.
    - Example: A digital marketing agency adopts rotational leadership roles to enhance team agility.
8. Recognition and Reward Systems: Establish systems to recognize and reward achievements.
    - Example: A retail chain launches a peer-recognition program to boost teamwork and customer service.
9. Inclusive Forums: Hold regular forums to ensure all voices are heard.
    - Example: A publishing house conducts monthly forums for idea-sharing and feedback.

10. Advanced Communication Tools: Upgrade communication tools to support real-time collaboration.
    - Example: A logistics company implements instant messaging and project management software to enhance real-time updates.

Conclusion

The "Himalayan Huddle" embodies a comprehensive approach to team dynamics, drawing from the strength and majesty of the Himalayas to build teams that are resilient, adaptive, and unified in their pursuits. By implementing these principles, organizations can achieve heightened synergy, drive innovation, and navigate the complexities of the business landscape effectively.

By integrating these principles, businesses can align their team dynamics with the unity and resilience symbolized by the Himalayas, ensuring that teams function as cohesive, high-performing units. This holistic approach fosters a culture of mutual trust, continuous learning, and strategic foresight, empowering teams to achieve collective goals and drive organizational success.

Complementary chapter:
Kashmir Shaivism and Corporate Shaivism

Sanskrit Shloka

Shiva Sutras 1.1:

शिवसूत्र 1.1:

"चैतन्यमात्मा"

Caitanyamātmā (Consciousness is the Self)

Translation

The foundational teaching here is that consciousness itself is the essence of the Self. This principle asserts that everything in existence, including our thoughts, actions, and decisions, arises from a universal consciousness.

Philosophical Context

In Kashmir Shaivism, Caitanyamātmā encapsulates the idea that the universe is a manifestation of pure consciousness. This non-dualistic perspective posits that the individual self (Atman) and the universal self (Brahman) are one and the same. By understanding this unity, one can transcend the illusion of separateness and recognize the divine in every aspect of life.

Business Use Cases

1. Mindful Leadership:
   - Theoretical Application: Leaders who embrace the concept of Caitanyamātmā recognize the interconnectedness of all

beings. This awareness fosters a leadership style rooted in compassion, empathy, and ethical integrity.
- Practical Implementation: Companies can institute regular mindfulness training for leaders to enhance their awareness and decision-making skills. These practices help in developing a work culture that values holistic well-being and ethical practices.
- Spiritual Connection: Mindful leadership aligns with the spiritual principle of seeing the divine in every individual, promoting a harmonious and respectful workplace.

2. Ethical Decision-Making:
   - Theoretical Application: Ethical decision-making arises naturally when one acknowledges the divine consciousness in all actions. Decisions are made not just for personal or corporate gain but for the greater good of all stakeholders.
   - Practical Implementation: Establishing a code of ethics grounded in the recognition of universal consciousness can guide business practices. Regular ethics workshops and an emphasis on transparency can reinforce this principle.
   - Spiritual Connection: Ethical decision-making is a reflection of spiritual integrity, ensuring that actions are in harmony with the greater good and universal laws.

3. Employee Empowerment:
   - Theoretical Application: Recognizing the divine in each employee encourages a culture of mutual respect and empowerment. Employees feel valued not just as workers but as integral parts of the organizational consciousness.
   - Practical Implementation: Implement policies that promote inclusivity, personal growth, and recognition. Programs

like peer recognition, leadership training, and personal development plans can foster a sense of empowerment.
- Spiritual Connection: Employee empowerment reflects the spiritual practice of honoring the divine spark within each person, fostering an environment of mutual respect and growth.

Detailed Explanation

Section 1: Introduction to Caitanyamātmā

- Definition and Importance: Caitanyamātmā, the concept that consciousness is the self, is central to understanding the non-dualistic nature of existence. This principle implies that every individual action and decision is an expression of the universal consciousness.
- Philosophical Roots: In Kashmir Shaivism, the recognition of the self as pure consciousness dissolves the illusion of separateness. This realization leads to a life of higher purpose and integrity.
- Spiritual Insight: Recognizing that consciousness pervades all actions encourages a sense of unity and interconnectedness, fostering a more compassionate and ethical approach to business.

Section 2: Mindful Leadership

- Case Study: Consider a tech company where the CEO practices mindfulness. By integrating mindfulness into daily routines and decision-making processes, the company has seen a reduction in stress levels and an increase in creative problem-solving.

- Techniques for Leaders: Techniques such as meditation, reflective journaling, and conscious breathing exercises can help leaders cultivate mindfulness. Leaders can also participate in retreats and workshops to deepen their practice.
- Spiritual Insight: Mindful leadership promotes the spiritual principle of living with awareness and intention, ensuring that actions are aligned with higher values and the well-being of all.

Section 3: Ethical Decision-Making

- Case Study: A manufacturing company that adopted a code of ethics based on recognizing the divine in all actions saw a significant improvement in stakeholder trust and a reduction in regulatory issues.
- Frameworks for Ethics: Developing a robust ethical framework involves creating guidelines that prioritize transparency, fairness, and accountability. Regular audits and feedback mechanisms ensure these practices are upheld.
- Spiritual Insight: Ethical decision-making is a reflection of spiritual integrity, ensuring that actions are in harmony with the greater good and universal laws.

Section 4: Employee Empowerment

- Case Study: A global consulting firm introduced a program where employees are encouraged to pursue personal development goals. This program includes mentorship, skills training, and wellness initiatives, leading to increased job satisfaction and retention.
- Empowerment Strategies: Strategies to empower employees include offering continuous learning opportunities, fostering open communication, and recognizing individual

contributions. Leadership should also encourage autonomy and creativity in problem-solving.
- **Spiritual Insight:** Employee empowerment reflects the spiritual practice of honoring the divine spark within each person, fostering an environment of mutual respect and growth.

🖤 Understanding the Power of Will
Sanskrit Shloka

Shiva Sutras 1.5:

शिवसूत्र 1.5:

"उद्यमो भैरवः"

Udyamo bhairavaḥ* (The rising will is Bhairava)

Translation

This verse highlights the power of will, equating it with Bhairava, a form of Shiva representing the transformative force of the universe. It emphasizes that a determined and focused willpower is akin to harnessing a divine energy.

Philosophical Context

In the context of Kashmir Shaivism, Bhairava represents the dynamic aspect of consciousness that brings about transformation and creation. Udyamo bhairavaḥ signifies the awakening of this dynamic force within oneself. It is through the exercise of willpower that one can manifest desires and overcome obstacles, leading to personal and professional fulfillment.

Business Use Cases

1. Goal Setting and Achievement:
   - Theoretical Application: The principle of Udyamo bhairavaḥ underscores the importance of setting clear, achievable goals and pursuing them with unwavering determination. This divine willpower ensures that goals are met despite challenges.
   - Practical Implementation: Businesses can incorporate goal-setting workshops and provide tools such as SMART goals frameworks to help employees set and achieve their objectives.
   - Spiritual Connection: Goal setting and achievement reflect the spiritual practice of harnessing one's divine will to manifest intentions and create positive change.

2. Innovation and Creativity:
   - Theoretical Application: Willpower drives innovation by pushing the boundaries of what is possible. Employees who harness this inner drive can think outside the box and develop groundbreaking solutions.
   - Practical Implementation: Encouraging a culture of experimentation and risk-taking can foster innovation. This can be supported by providing resources for research and development and celebrating successful innovations.
   - Spiritual Connection: Innovation and creativity are expressions of the divine will in action, reflecting the transformative power of Bhairava within each individual.

3. Overcoming Challenges:
   - Theoretical Application: A strong willpower enables individuals and organizations to navigate through crises

and challenges effectively. This resilience is rooted in the belief that obstacles are opportunities for growth and transformation.
- Practical Implementation: Training programs focused on building resilience and stress management can prepare employees to handle challenges. Developing contingency plans and fostering a supportive work environment also contribute to overcoming obstacles.
- Spiritual Connection: Overcoming challenges through willpower is a testament to the spiritual principle of embracing transformation and growth as part of the divine journey.

Detailed Explanation

Section 1: Introduction to Udyamo Bhairavaḥ

- Definition and Importance: Udyamo bhairavaḥ emphasizes the transformative power of will. Recognizing this principle enables individuals to harness their inner strength and drive to achieve their goals.
- Philosophical Roots: In Kashmir Shaivism, Bhairava is not just a deity but a symbol of the potent energy within every individual. Awakening this energy through willpower leads to personal and professional transformation.
- Spiritual Insight: Understanding willpower as a divine force encourages individuals to approach their goals with a sense of purpose and determination, seeing their efforts as part of a larger spiritual journey.

Section 2: Goal Setting and Achievement

- Case Study: A financial services firm implemented a comprehensive goal-setting program that included regular check-ins and accountability measures. This approach resulted in a significant increase in employee performance and company profits.
- Practical Tools: Tools such as the SMART goals framework, vision boards, and regular performance reviews can help employees set and achieve their goals. Encouraging a culture of accountability and celebration of achievements also reinforces this practice.
- Spiritual Insight: Setting and achieving goals is seen as an alignment with one's higher purpose, where each accomplishment is a step toward fulfilling one's divine potential.

Section 3: Innovation and Creativity

- Case Study: A tech startup that encouraged a culture of innovation by providing dedicated time and resources for employees to work on passion projects. This led to the development of several successful new products.
- Fostering Innovation: To foster innovation, businesses can create innovation labs, hold hackathons, and provide grants or rewards for innovative ideas. Encouraging cross-functional collaboration and diverse thinking also sparks creativity.
- Spiritual Insight: Innovation is viewed as the manifestation of the divine will in action, where creative solutions and breakthroughs are seen as expressions of the transformative power of consciousness.

Section 4: Overcoming Challenges

- Case Study : A healthcare organization that faced a major crisis used resilience training and a strong support system to navigate through the challenges successfully. This approach led to improved patient care and staff morale.
- Building Resilience: Developing a culture that values resilience involves providing stress management resources, encouraging open communication, and creating a supportive work environment. Leaders should model resilience and provide mentorship to help employees develop these skills.
- Spiritual Insight: Overcoming challenges through willpower reflects the spiritual journey of growth and transformation, where each obstacle is an opportunity to realize one's divine potential and strength.

CHAPTER 21

FOCUS ON INNER STRENGTH AND KNOWLEDGE

Sanskrit Shloka

Spanda Kārikās 1.5:

स्पन्दकारिकास 1.5:

"स्वातन्त्र्यम् विश्वसिद्धिदम्"

Svātantryam visva-siddhidam (Freedom brings about universal accomplishment)

Translation

This verse highlights the power of inner freedom and self-reliance. It suggests that true success and accomplishment arise from within and are achieved through the exercise of personal freedom and autonomy.

Philosophical Context

The concept of Svātantryam in Kashmir Shaivism refers to the ultimate freedom of the self, unbound by external limitations. This freedom is the source of creativity, innovation, and the ability to achieve universal accomplishments. By embracing self-reliance, individuals and organizations can tap into their inherent potential and achieve remarkable success.

Business Use Cases

1. Innovation through Autonomy:
   - Theoretical Application: Autonomy fosters a sense of ownership and responsibility, leading to increased innovation and creativity. When employees are given the freedom to explore and experiment, they are more likely to develop innovative solutions.
   - Practical Implementation: Creating a work environment that values autonomy involves providing flexible work arrangements, encouraging independent thinking, and supporting employee-led initiatives.
   - Spiritual Connection: Innovation through autonomy aligns with the spiritual principle of self-reliance, where individuals harness their inner freedom to create and innovate.
2. Empowered Leadership:
   - Theoretical Application: Leaders who focus on inner strength and knowledge can inspire and guide their teams more effectively. This empowerment stems from a deep understanding of their own potential and the ability to foster growth in others.

- Practical Implementation: Leadership development programs that focus on self-awareness, emotional intelligence, and continuous learning can cultivate empowered leaders. Providing opportunities for leaders to engage in personal development and reflective practices enhances their ability to lead with wisdom and strength.
- Spiritual Connection: Empowered leadership reflects the spiritual practice of nurturing one's inner strength and knowledge, guiding others with wisdom and compassion.

3. Resilient Organizations:
   - Theoretical Application: Businesses that cultivate self-reliance are more resilient and adaptable to changes and challenges. This inner strength allows organizations to navigate uncertainty with confidence and agility.
   - Practical Implementation: Building a resilient organization involves fostering a culture of continuous learning, encouraging adaptability, and developing strong support systems. Providing resources for professional development and creating an environment that values flexibility and innovation contribute to organizational resilience.
   - Spiritual Connection: Resilient organizations embody the spiritual principle of embracing inner strength and freedom, adapting to change with grace and confidence.

Detailed Explanation

Section 1: Introduction to Svātantryam Visva-Siddhidam

- Definition and Importance: Understanding the concept of inner freedom and its role in achieving success. This principle

emphasizes the importance of self-reliance and autonomy in personal and professional growth.
- Philosophical Roots: In Kashmir Shaivism, Svātantryam represents the ultimate freedom of the self, unbound by external limitations. This freedom is the source of creativity, innovation, and universal accomplishment.
- Spiritual Insight: Embracing inner freedom allows individuals to tap into their divine potential, fostering creativity and innovation as expressions of their true nature.

Section 2: Innovation through Autonomy

- Case Study: A tech company that implemented a flexible work policy allowing employees to pursue personal projects. This approach led to several successful innovations and increased employee satisfaction.
- Fostering Autonomy: Encouraging autonomy involves providing flexible work arrangements, supporting independent thinking, and fostering a culture of trust. Regular check-ins and feedback mechanisms ensure that employees feel supported while maintaining their autonomy.
- Spiritual Insight: Innovation through autonomy reflects the spiritual principle of self-reliance, where individuals harness their inner freedom to create and innovate, contributing to the greater good.

Section 3: Empowered Leadership

- Case Study: A global corporation that invested in leadership development programs focusing on emotional intelligence and self-awareness. This approach led to more effective and

compassionate leadership, improving overall organizational performance.
- Cultivating Empowerment: Leadership development programs that emphasize self-awareness, emotional intelligence, and continuous learning can cultivate empowered leaders. Providing opportunities for leaders to engage in personal development and reflective practices enhances their ability to lead with wisdom and strength.
- Spiritual Insight: Empowered leadership reflects the spiritual practice of nurturing one's inner strength and knowledge, guiding others with wisdom and compassion, and fostering a culture of growth and empowerment.

Section 4: Resilient Organizations

- Case Study: A manufacturing company that developed a robust professional development program, encouraging employees to continuously learn and adapt. This approach resulted in increased resilience and adaptability in the face of market changes.
- Building Resilience: Developing a resilient organization involves fostering a culture of continuous learning, encouraging adaptability, and developing strong support systems. Providing resources for professional development and creating an environment that values flexibility and innovation contribute to organizational resilience.
- Spiritual Insight: Resilient organizations embody the spiritual principle of embracing inner strength and freedom, adapting to change with grace and confidence, and viewing challenges as opportunities for growth.

💜 The Role of Self-Reflection

Sanskrit Shloka

Pratyabhijna Hridayam 17:

प्रत्यभिज्ञा हृदयम् 17:

"चैतन्यमात्मास्फुरत्ता"

Caitanyam-ātmā-sphurattā (Consciousness is the pulsation of the Self)

Translation

This verse emphasizes the dynamic and pulsating nature of consciousness. It suggests that self-awareness and reflection are key to understanding one's true nature.

Philosophical Context

In Kashmir Shaivism, Caitanyam-ātmā-sphurattā highlights the ever-vibrant and dynamic aspect of consciousness. This pulsation signifies the constant flow and evolution of awareness. By engaging in self-reflection, one can align with this dynamic consciousness, leading to greater self-understanding and authentic living.

Business Use Cases

1. Strategic Planning:
   - Theoretical Application: Regular self-reflection helps businesses align their strategies with their core values and mission. By understanding the pulsating nature of consciousness, businesses can adapt and evolve in alignment with their true purpose.

- Practical Implementation: Incorporating reflective practices such as SWOT analysis, strategic retreats, and regular feedback loops can enhance strategic planning. Ensuring that the organization's mission and values are central to the planning process helps maintain alignment and authenticity.
- Spiritual Connection: Strategic planning through self-reflection aligns with the spiritual practice of staying connected to one's true nature and purpose, ensuring that actions are in harmony with higher values.

2. Leadership Development:
   - Theoretical Application: Leaders who practice self-reflection are more effective and adaptive. This practice allows them to understand their strengths and areas for growth, fostering continuous improvement and authentic leadership.
   - Practical Implementation: Leadership development programs that incorporate reflective practices, such as journaling, meditation, and peer feedback, can enhance self-awareness and adaptability. Encouraging leaders to engage in regular self-assessment and continuous learning supports their development.
   - Spiritual Connection: Leadership development through self-reflection reflects the spiritual journey of self-awareness and growth, where leaders align their actions with their higher purpose and values.

3. Continuous Improvement:
   - Theoretical Application: A culture of self-reflection encourages continuous improvement and learning. By

regularly assessing processes and outcomes, businesses can identify areas for enhancement and innovation.

- Practical Implementation: Implementing continuous improvement programs such as Kaizen, Six Sigma, and regular performance reviews fosters a culture of learning and growth. Encouraging employees to engage in reflective practices and seek feedback supports continuous improvement.
- Spiritual Connection: Continuous improvement through self-reflection embodies the spiritual principle of evolving and growing in alignment with one's true nature, where each step is seen as part of the journey toward greater fulfillment and excellence.

Detailed Explanation

Section 1: Introduction to Caitanyam-ātmā-sphurattā

- Definition and Importance: Caitanyam-ātmā-sphurattā highlights the dynamic and pulsating nature of consciousness. This principle emphasizes the importance of self-awareness and reflection in understanding and aligning with one's true nature.
- Philosophical Roots: In Kashmir Shaivism, the pulsation of consciousness represents the constant flow and evolution of awareness. Engaging in self-reflection allows individuals to align with this dynamic consciousness, leading to greater self-understanding and authentic living.
- Spiritual Insight: Recognizing the dynamic nature of consciousness encourages a practice of regular self-reflection, fostering a deeper connection to one's true self and purpose.

Section 2: Strategic Planning

- Case Study: A global non-profit organization that integrated reflective practices into its strategic planning process. By regularly assessing its mission and values, the organization was able to adapt and evolve in alignment with its core purpose, leading to greater impact and sustainability.
- Reflective Practices: Incorporating practices such as SWOT analysis, strategic retreats, and regular feedback loops can enhance strategic planning. Ensuring that the organization's mission and values are central to the planning process helps maintain alignment and authenticity.
- Spiritual Insight: Strategic planning through self-reflection aligns with the spiritual practice of staying connected to one's true nature and purpose, ensuring that actions are in harmony with higher values and the greater good.

Section 3: Leadership Development

- Case Study: A multinational corporation that implemented a leadership development program focusing on self-reflection and continuous learning. This approach resulted in more adaptive and authentic leadership, improving overall organizational performance and employee engagement.
- Reflective Practices: Leadership development programs that incorporate reflective practices, such as journaling, meditation, and peer feedback, can enhance self-awareness and adaptability. Encouraging leaders to engage in regular self-assessment and continuous learning supports their development and growth.
- Spiritual Insight: Leadership development through self-reflection reflects the spiritual journey of self-awareness and

growth, where leaders align their actions with their higher purpose and values, fostering a culture of authenticity and compassion.

Section 4: Continuous Improvement

- Case Study: A technology company that adopted a continuous improvement program based on regular self-assessment and feedback. This approach led to significant process improvements, innovation, and increased customer satisfaction.
- Implementing Continuous Improvement: Implementing continuous improvement programs such as Kaizen, Six Sigma, and regular performance reviews fosters a culture of learning and growth. Encouraging employees to engage in reflective practices and seek feedback supports continuous improvement and innovation.
- Spiritual Insight: Continuous improvement through self-reflection embodies the spiritual principle of evolving and growing in alignment with one's true nature, where each step is seen as part of the journey toward greater fulfillment and excellence, contributing to the overall well-being of the organization and its stakeholders.

♥ Balancing Dualities
Sanskrit Shloka

Vijnana Bhairava Tantra 101:

विज्ञान भैरव तन्त्र 101:

"द्वन्द्वानि गतयस्तेषां तत्त्वे तत्त्वं विलक्षयेत्"

Dvandvāni gatayasteṣāṁ tattve tattvaṁ vilakṣayet (One should identify the reality in all opposing elements)

Translation

This verse advises us to see the underlying reality beyond apparent dualities and conflicts. It promotes a balanced approach to life and business.

Philosophical Context

In Kashmir Shaivism, the recognition of dualities and the underlying unity is essential for achieving a balanced and harmonious existence. Dvandvāni gatayasteṣāṁ tattve tattvaṁ vilakṣayet suggests that by seeing beyond the surface-level oppositions, one can understand the deeper reality and achieve a state of equilibrium.

Business Use Cases

1. Conflict Resolution:
   - Theoretical Application: Businesses that recognize and address the underlying realities in conflicts can resolve issues more effectively. Understanding the deeper connections between seemingly opposing forces leads to harmonious resolutions.
   - Practical Implementation: Implementing conflict resolution strategies such as mediation, active listening, and collaborative problem-solving can help address underlying issues. Providing training in conflict resolution and creating a culture of open communication supports this process.

- Spiritual Connection: Conflict resolution through understanding dualities reflects the spiritual practice of seeing unity in diversity, fostering harmony and collaboration in the workplace.
2. Balanced Decision-Making:
    - Theoretical Application: A balanced approach to decision-making leads to more sustainable and equitable outcomes. By recognizing the underlying unity in dualities, businesses can make decisions that consider multiple perspectives and long-term impacts.
    - Practical Implementation: Decision-making frameworks such as the balanced scorecard, scenario planning, and stakeholder analysis can help ensure a holistic approach. Encouraging diverse viewpoints and considering both short-term and long-term impacts supports balanced decision-making.
    - Spiritual Connection: Balanced decision-making aligns with the spiritual principle of integrating multiple perspectives, ensuring that actions are in harmony with the greater good and long-term sustainability.
3. Holistic Management:
    - Theoretical Application: Understanding the interconnectedness of different aspects of business promotes holistic management practices. This approach ensures that all elements of the organization work together harmoniously toward common goals.
    - Practical Implementation: Implementing holistic management practices such as integrated reporting, systems thinking, and cross-functional collaboration can enhance organizational effectiveness. Encouraging a culture of

continuous improvement and alignment with core values supports holistic management.
- Spiritual Connection: Holistic management embodies the spiritual practice of recognizing the interconnectedness of all things, ensuring that organizational practices are aligned with higher values and contribute to the overall well-being of all stakeholders.

Detailed Explanation

Section 1: Introduction to Dvandvāni gatayasteṣāṁ tattve tattvaṁ vilakṣayet

- Definition and Importance: Understanding the concept of dualities and their implications for business. This principle emphasizes the importance of recognizing the underlying unity in apparent oppositions, leading to balanced and harmonious outcomes.
- Philosophical Roots: In Kashmir Shaivism, the recognition of dualities and the underlying unity is essential for achieving a balanced and harmonious existence. This principle guides individuals to see beyond surface-level conflicts and understand the deeper reality.
- Spiritual Insight: Recognizing the underlying unity in dualities fosters a balanced and harmonious approach to life and business, promoting collaboration and mutual understanding.

Section 2: Conflict Resolution

- Case Study: A multinational company that implemented a comprehensive conflict resolution program focusing on mediation and active listening. This approach led to more

effective resolution of conflicts, improved employee relations, and a more harmonious work environment.
- Conflict Resolution Strategies: Implementing conflict resolution strategies such as mediation, active listening, and collaborative problem-solving can help address underlying issues. Providing training in conflict resolution and creating a culture of open communication supports this process.
- Spiritual Insight: Conflict resolution through understanding dualities reflects the spiritual practice of seeing unity in diversity, fostering harmony and collaboration in the workplace, and contributing to a positive organizational culture.

Section 3: Balanced Decision-Making

- Case Study: A financial services firm that adopted a balanced decision-making framework, considering both short-term and long-term impacts. This approach led to more sustainable and equitable outcomes, benefiting both the organization and its stakeholders.
- Decision-Making Frameworks: Decision-making frameworks such as the balanced scorecard, scenario planning, and stakeholder analysis can help ensure a holistic approach. Encouraging diverse viewpoints and considering both short-term and long-term impacts supports balanced decision-making.
- Spiritual Insight: Balanced decision-making aligns with the spiritual principle of integrating multiple perspectives, ensuring that actions are in harmony with the greater good and long-term sustainability, fostering a culture of wisdom and integrity.

Section 4: Holistic Management

- Case Study: A healthcare organization that implemented holistic management practices, focusing on integrated reporting and cross-functional collaboration. This approach enhanced organizational effectiveness, improved patient outcomes, and fostered a culture of continuous improvement.
- Holistic Management Practices: Implementing holistic management practices such as integrated reporting, systems thinking, and cross-functional collaboration can enhance organizational effectiveness. Encouraging a culture of continuous improvement and alignment with core values supports holistic management.
- Spiritual Insight: Holistic management embodies the spiritual practice of recognizing the interconnectedness of all things, ensuring that organizational practices are aligned with higher values and contribute to the overall well-being of all stakeholders, fostering a culture of compassion and excellence.

www.ingramcontent.com/pod-product-compliance
Lightning Source LLC
LaVergne TN
LVHW061613070526
838199LV00078B/7269